INTRODUCTION TO U.S. ENVIRONMENTAL LAWS

by Edward E. Shea

OCEANA PUBLICATIONS, INC.
NEW YORK • LONDON • ROME

Library of Congress Cataloging in Publication Data

Introduction to U.S. Environmental Laws. Shea, Edward E.

ISBN: 0-379-21353-2

Published by Oceana Publications, Inc.

Manufactured in the United States of America on acid-free paper.

About the Author

Edward E. Shea is a partner in the law firm of Windels, Marx, Davies & Ives in New York City, and is responsible for its enviromental practice. He received his J.D. at the University of Michigan and his B.A. at the University of Detroit.

Mr. Shea has held executive positions with the GAF Corporation and Reichhold Chemicals, Inc. Since 1988 the author has been corporate secretary and counsel to the Peridot Chemicals Group. In addition to writing several books on business topics, Mr. Shea has published a number of articles in such journals as: *Environmental Compliance & Litigation Strategy, Environmental Management Review, ABA Journal, The New York Law Journal, and the National Law Journal.*

INTRODUCTION TO U.S. ENVIRONMENTAL LAWS

TABLE OF CONTENTS

I. OVERVIEW 1

II. LAWS REGULATING NAVIGABLE WATERS AND HAR-
BOR AND RIVER IMPROVEMENTS 2

III. NATIONAL ENVIRONMENTAL POLICY ACT 3

IV. THE CLEAN AIR ACT 5

  A. Legislative History 5
  B. Ambient Air Quality 7
    (i) Air Quality Control Regions 7
    (ii) State Implementation Plans 7
    (iii) Nonattainment Areas 8
    (iv) Prevention of Significant Deterioration 9
  C. New Source Performance Standards 10
  D. National Emission Standards for Hazardous Air Pollutants . 10
    (i) Pre-1990 NESHAPs 10
    (ii) Post-1990 NESHAPs 11
    (iii) Major Sources 11
    (iv) Area Sources 12
    (v)Technology-Based Standards for NESHAPS 12
    (vi) Health-Based Standards for NESHAPs 13
    (vii) Accidental Releases 13
    (viii) Court Review of HAP Listing 14
  E. Motor Vehicles and Clean Fuels 15

F. Acid Deposition Control (Acid Rain) 15
G. Stratospheric Ozone Provisions 17
H. Permits 18
I. Enforcement 20

V. CLEAN WATER ACT 21

A. General 21
B. Effluent Standards 21
C. Water Quality Standards 24
D. NPDES Program and Permits 24
E. Nonpointsource Effluent 25
F. Stormwater 26
G. Spills 26
H. Wetlands 27
I. Sewage Sludge 27

VI. RESOURCE CONSERVATION AND RECOVERY ACT 28

A. General 28
B. Solid Waste 28
C. Hazardous Waste 29
D. Recycling, Reclamation and Reuse 30
E. Generator Responsibilities 31
F. Transporter Responsibilities 31
G. TSD Facilities 31
H. Underground Storage Tanks 32
I. "Land Ban" Regulations 33
J. Medical Waste 34

**VII. THE COMPREHENSIVE ENVIRONMENTAL RESPONSE,
COMPENSATION AND LIABILITY ACT** 34

A. General 34

B. Definition of a Hazardous Substance 35
C. Releases 36
D. Removal Actions 36
E. The National Contingency Plan 36
F. The National Priority List 37
G. Remedial Actions 37
H. Steps to Accomplish Remediation 38
I. Remedy Selection Standards ("How Clean is Clean") 40
J. Recovery of Response Costs 42
K. Contribution Rights 45
L. The CERCLA Lien 45
M. Lender Liability 46
N. Parent Corporation and Shareholder Liability 47
O. Officer and Director Liability 47
P. Successor Liability 48
Q. Arranger and Transporter Liability 48
R. Indemnification 49
S. Pending Legislation 49

VIII. EMERGENCY PLANNING AND COMMUNITY
RIGHT-TO-KNOW ACT 53

IX. THE TOXIC SUBSTANCES CONTROL ACT 55

X. LAWS RELATING TO ASBESTOS CONTAINING
MATERIALS 59

XI. THE SAFE DRINKING WATER ACT 62

XII. FEDERAL INSECTICIDE, FUNGICIDE AND
RODENTICIDE ACT 65

XIII. HAZARDOUS MATERIALS TRANSPORTATION ACT 69

XIV. MARINE PROTECTION, RESEARCH AND
SANCTUARIES ACT 71

XV. OCCUPATIONAL SAFETY AND HEALTH ACT 72

A. General 72
B. National Consensus Standards 73
C. Safety Standards 73
D. Health Standards 73
E. Air Contaminants Standard 74
F. Chemical Process Standard 74
G. Hazardous Waste Operations 75
H. Bloodborne Pathogens Standard 75
I. Penalties 75
J. State Administration 76
K. The Role of OSHA 76

XVI. LAWS RELATING TO LEAD 77

A. Clean Air Act 78
B. Clean Water Act 78
C. Safe Drinking Water Act 78
D. Resource Conservation and Recovery Act 79
E. CERCLA 79
F. Occupational Safety and Health Act 79
G. Consumer Product Safety Act 80
H. Toxic Substances Control Act 80
I. Lead-Based Paint Poisoning Prevention Act, 42 U.S.C.
§ 4801 and the Residential Lead-Based Paint Reduction Act,
42 U.S.C.§ 4851. 81
J. State Environmental and Health Laws 82
K. Lead-Based Paint Litigation 83

XVII. THE OIL POLLUTION ACT 84

    A. Liability Provisions 84
    B. Financial Responsibility 86
    C. The Oil Spill Liability Fund 87
    D. Prevention of Oil Pollution 87
    E. Removal of Oil Discharges 88
    F. Regulations 88

XVIII. LAWS PROTECTING WILDLIFE, FISH, PLANTS AND MARINE MAMMALS 88

    A. The Endangered Species Act 88
    B. The Marine Mammal Protection Act 90
    C. Related Laws 91

XIX. NOISE CONTROL LAWS 91

XX. LAWS GOVERNING RADIOACTIVE MATERIALS AND WASTES 92

XXI. OTHER FEDERAL ENVIRONMENTAL LAWS 98

XXII. LIMITATIONS IMPOSED BY THE U.S. CONSTITUTION 98

XXIII. STATE LAWS 100

    A. State General Environmental Laws 100
    B. State Real Property Transfer Laws 102

XXIV. FUTURE TRENDS 104

XXV. CONCLUSION 106

INTRODUCTION TO U.S. ENVIRONMENTAL LAWS

I. OVERVIEW

The major environmental laws in the United States are federal laws administered primarily by the Environmental Protection Agency (USEPA). However, much of the administration of these laws has been delegated to those states which have adopted and implemented laws at least as strict as the federal laws. When administration is delegated, the USEPA continues to support administration with funding, research, development of standards and methods, and a secondary enforcement role. Local government units (such as regions, counties and cities) also have laws which supplement, but cannot contradict, the federal and state laws. The states and many municipalities also have many environmental laws which are not part of the federal pattern.

The environmental laws are lengthy and detailed. The federal laws alone total thousands of pages. The USEPA's regulations interpreting and implementing the federal laws total many thousands of pages including lists of chemical substances and their characteristics, test methods and equipment, and control methods and equipment.

Each law has its own enforcement provisions and civil and criminal penalties. In general, the laws require record keeping and periodic reporting, provide for inspections, and impose civil and criminal fines and jail terms for violations. They are strictly enforced, primarily by orders for compliance and corrective action. However, civil penalties and fines are frequently imposed. Criminal actions are less common, but relatively frequent. Jail terms are reserved for the most serious cases.

Many environmental laws also allow private citizens and groups to file lawsuits for enforcement and to obtain money damages. Many of these lawsuits are successful. Thus, compliance with government programs is not always the end of environmental responsibilities.

1

Factors stimulating adoption of environmental laws have included scientific advancements in analytical chemistry, computer and communications technology, and toxicology. Development of analytical equipment such as chromatographs and spectrophotometers made possible the detection of contaminants at parts per trillion and lower. Computer and communications advances made it possible to collect data from widespread sources and rapidly analyze and distribute the results throughout the United States. Using these advances, the field of toxicology (including risk assessment) has grown into a major field. Environmental engineering, geology, industrial hygiene and law have also grown from courses into major fields taught at universities and practiced in specialized firms and in departments of government agencies and large companies.

II. LAWS REGULATING NAVIGABLE WATERS AND HARBOR AND RIVER IMPROVEMENTS

The Rivers and Harbors Act of 1899 (sometimes called the Refuse Act), 33 U.S.C. § 407, was for decades the only federal environmental law restricting the discharge of pollutants that was not primarily directed to safety. The Refuse Act prohibits the discharge or deposit of refuse, other than liquid flows from streets and sewers, into any navigable water (or tributary) of the United States. Refuse is any substance not naturally occurring in the water. The courts have consistently found that waste from industrial processes, such as taconite tailings, are refuse. *Reserve Mining Co. v. Environmental Protection Agency*, 514 F.2d 492 (8th Cir. 1975). Violations are punishable by fines up to $2,500 and a jail term up to one year. The Refuse Act authorizes the U.S. Army Corps of Engineers to permit the deposit of any material in navigable waters within limits and under conditions prescribed by the Corps of Engineers. Most courts have ruled that private individuals do not have rights to sue under the Refuse Act. *National Sea Clammers Ass'n. v. New York*, 616 F.2d 1222 (3d Cir. 1980) and cases cited therein; *Yates v. Island Creek Coal Co.*, 485 F. Supp. 995 (W.D. Va. 1980). The Act has been partially preempted or supplemented by later federal environmental laws. *U.S. v. M/V Big Sam*, 681 F.2d 432 (5th Cir. 1982); *U.S. v. Outboard Marine Corp.*, 789 F.2d 497 (7th Cir. 1986).

A series of statutory provisions found at 33 U.S.C. § 401 *et seq.* restrict construction, dredging, filling and other activities in navigable waters of the United States without the approval of the U.S. Army Corps of Engineers and, in some cases, other governmental authorities such as the U.S. Secretary of Transportation. The regulations of the Corps of Engineers are at 33 C.F.R. Part 203 *et seq.* Of important environmental interest are its regulations on general regulatory policies (Part 320), permits (Parts 321 to 330), and projects involving the discharge of dredged or fill material (Parts 335 and 336). Many lawsuits have been brought against the Corps of Engineers by environmental groups who believed that various permits were granted without sufficient consideration of environmental effects. See, e.g., *Sierra Club v. Morton*, 451 U.S. 287; *Roanoke River Basin Ass'n v. Hudson*, 940 F.2d 58 (4th Cir. 1991); *Van Abbema v. Farnell*, 807 F.2d 633 (7th Cir. 1986). Property owners and developers have also engaged in litigation with the Corps of Engineers, contending that it gave too much consideration to environmental effects in exercising its authority to deny, restrict or enforce permits. See, e.g., *Fox Bay Partners v. U.S. Corps of Engineers*, 831 F.Supp. 605 (N.D. Ill. 1993); *United States v. Members of the Estate of Boothby*, 16 F.3d 19 (1st Cir. 1994).

III. NATIONAL ENVIRONMENTAL POLICY ACT

The National Environmental Policy Act (NEPA), 42 U.S.C. § 4321 *et seq.*, was adopted in 1970. It established a national environmental policy and goals stated in broad terms. It also established the Council on Environmental Quality (CEQ).

With some exceptions, NEPA requires that all federal government agencies prepare an environmental impact statement (EIS) for every proposal of a major federal action significantly affecting the human environment. Where several agencies are involved, a lead agency assumes primary responsibility. The procedures involve preparation of a preliminary EIS, usually containing extensive data furnished by the company applying for a permit or seeking other major action being considered by the agency. Public hearings are held and further information is obtained resulting in the preparation of a final EIS. News media often report the ongoing events. The

CEQ regulations governing EISs are found at 40 C.F.R. Part 1500 *et seq*. Related USEPA regulations are at 40 C.F.R. Part 6.

NEPA does not apply if an agency finds that a proposed action is not major or has no significant impact on the environment. Environmentalists can challenge the finding and other failures to comply with NEPA if they would be injured by the agency's failure. However, the U.S. Supreme Court has ruled that an agency's final decision cannot be challenged if it has complied with NEPA procedures and its decision is not arbitrary or capricious. *Marsh v. Oregon Natural Resources Council*, 490 U.S. 360 (1989); *Vermont Yankee Nuclear Corporation*, 435 U.S. 519 (1978).

Environmentalists who presented challenges at public hearings and commenced lawsuits challenging the adequacy of EIS information made NEPA into a significant environmental law. They vigorously opposed any perceived failure by a government agency to identify environmental concerns, describe fully the short and long term environmental impacts of the project, or consider fully all effective environmental controls. Federal actions such as highways, dams, bridges and power plants have been challenged by environmental groups alleging failure to consider effects on birds, fish and animals; wetlands; ancient burial grounds; noise levels; and the character of an area as a wilderness, forest or rural setting. For example, environmentalists achieved major victories restricting logging and selling of timber on grounds that the U.S. Forest Service failed to consider adequately the protection of the "spotted owl" as required by NEPA and the National Forrest Management Act, 16 U.S.C. § 1600 *et. seq.*, in spite of strong opposition by the timber industry and workers who would lose employment. See, e.g. *Seattle Audubon Society v. Espy*, 998 F.2d 699 (9th Cir. 1993).

An agency must (1) accurately identify the relevant environmental concern, (2) take a "hard look" at the problem, (3) if it finds no significant environmental impact, prepare a convincing case for its finding, and (4) if it finds an impact of true significance, prepare an EIS unless it finds that changes or safeguards in a project sufficiently reduce the impact to a minimum. *Sierra Club v. U.S. Dept. of Transportation*, 753 F.2d 120 (D.C. Cir. 1985). The agency must consider all reasonable alternatives, including a "no action" alternative. However, it need not use "worst case analysis" or analyze the environmental consequences of alternatives found too remote, speculative, impractical or ineffective. *Marsh v. Oregon Natural Resources Council*, 490 U.S. 360 (1989). *All Indian Pueblo Council v. U.S.*, 975 F.2d 1437 (10th Cir. 1992).

Environmental groups who have sued government agencies to require further and stricter actions under NEPA sometimes found that an agency would readily settle for a decree which expanded its authority. In 1994, a Circuit Court of Appeals allowed two timber industry trade associations to intervene in a lawsuit commenced by environmentalist groups against the Department of Agriculture after finding that the interests of the industry were not adequately represented. *Sierra Club v. Espy, Secretary of Agriculture*, 18 F.3d 1202 (5th Cir. 1994).

NEPA does not apply to state government agencies. However, some states have laws similar to NEPA. An example is the New York State Environmental Quality Review Act (SEQRA). New York Envtl. Conserv. Law § 8-0101 *et seq.* (McKinney 1984).

Both NEPA and the corresponding state laws are sometimes used by persons seeking a commercial objective. Commercial or industrial businesses may seek to prevent or delay the establishment of a new competitive business by claiming that government agencies considering permits should not grant them without requiring the applicant to go through EIS procedures. In 1993, for example, opponents of the North American Free Trade Agreement sought unsuccessfully to block that treaty because an EIS had not been prepared. *Public Citizen v. U.S. Trade Representative*, 5 F.3d 549 (D.C. Cir. 1993); *see also Public Citizen v. Office of the U.S. Trade Representative*, 970 F.2d 916 (D.C. Cir. 1992).

IV. THE CLEAN AIR ACT

A.   Legislative History

The Clean Air Act (CAA), 42 U.S.C. § 7401 *et seq.*, was adopted in 1963, but its provisions were then quite modest. In 1970, extensive amendments to the CAA were adopted. They provided for air quality control regions (AQCR), primary and secondary national ambient air quality standards (NAAQS), new source performance standards (NSPS), and national emission standards for hazardous air pollutants (NESHAPs).

The 1970 amendments also directed each state to adopt a state implementation plan (SIP) to attain the NAAQS; to regulate construction, modification and operation of specific pollution sources; to enforce emission limitations, and to establish monitoring and other programs. Each SIP, including amendments, must be approved by the USEPA and can be stricter, but not less strict, than the federal law and regulations. The USEPA was authorized to adopt a SIP, or a portion of a SIP, for any state not doing so. 42 U.S.C. § 7407 *et seq.*

In 1977 and 1982, amendments to the CAA required that the states add stricter requirements to their SIPs for prevention of significant deterioration (PSD) of air quality in areas which meet the NAAQS. 42 U.S.C. §§ 7471-7479. The amendments also established stricter requirements for major new sources of pollution in areas not attaining the NAAQS. 42 U.S.C. §§ 7501-7507.

The Clean Air Act Amendments of 1990 (CAAA of 1990) amended and extensively supplemented the CAA. Among other things, the CAAA of 1990 established stricter ambient air quality standards for nonattainment areas and new NAAQS compliance deadlines; major programs governing vehicles and fuels; an expanded program to establish NESHAPs for at least 189 air toxics; a program to reduce sulfur dioxide emissions by electric utilities perceived to be causing "acid rain"; an expanded permit program which state environmental agencies must adopt in their SIPs; a phaseout of chlorofluorocarbons (CFC) and certain other products perceived to deplete stratospheric ozone; new enforcement powers for the USEPA; stricter criminal and civil penalties for violation of the CAA; and a variety of programs including assistance to workers terminated or laid off as a consequence of compliance with the CAA.

B.   Ambient Air Quality

(i) *Air Quality Control Regions.* The USEPA has adopted 275 AQCR. 40 C.F.R. Part 81. The USEPA has also adopted national primary and secondary NAAQS for particulate matter, sulfur oxides, carbon monoxide, nitrogen dioxide, ozone and lead. 40 C.F.R. Part 50. The NAAQS are general air quality standards and do not apply to particular plants or equipment. They are implemented by the SIPs adopted by the states.

(ii) *State Implementation Plans.* The states adopted SIPs as required by Section 110 of the CAA, 42 U.S.C. § 7410, and the USEPA's regulations at 40 C.F.R. Part 51. The USEPA disapproved some SIP proposals and reassumed implementation where it believed the state program was inadequate.

The SIPs operated primarily through permit programs which limited emissions from specific stationary sources such as stacks, vents, pipes, tanks and boilers as well as fugitive emissions from sources such as equipment leaks and loading and unloading activities. The permits typically required monitoring, record keeping and reporting to the state environmental agency and were also enforced by surveillance and inspections. In addition to NAAQS and NESHAP pollutants, SIPs controlled volatile organic compounds and other pollutants from designated sources such as fluoride emissions from phosphate fertilizer and aluminum plants, sulfur emissions from kraft pulp mills and sulfuric acid mist from sulfuric acid production plants. 40 C.F.R. Parts 52 and 62.

The CAAA of 1990 established new uniform minimum standards for SIPs. Each SIP must be adopted after notice and a public hearing and must (A) contain enforceable emission limitations and other control measures; (B) provide for monitoring, compilation and analysis of ambient air quality data; (C) include an enforcement program and regulation of modification and construction of stationary sources including a permit program; (D) contain provisions prohibiting emissions of air pollutants in amounts which interfere with attainment or maintenance of the NAAQS, PSD or visibility requirements of any other state and insuring compliance with certain interstate and international pollution abatement require-

7

ments; (E) provide for adequate personnel, funding and authority and state responsibility for ensuring adequate implementation of SIP provisions delegated to local or regional authorities; (F) require monitoring and periodic reporting of emissions data; (G) provide authority comparable to the emergency powers of the USEPA relating to pollutant emissions presenting an imminent and substantial danger to public health or welfare or the environment and related contingency plans; (H) provide for revision of the SIP to take into account NAAQS revisions and other matters; (I) meet requirements applicable to nonattainment areas; (J) meet PSD and visibility requirements; (K) provide for air quality modelling and submission of data to the USEPA; (L) require permit fees payable by the owner or operator of each major stationary source; and (M) provide for consultation and participation by local political subdivisions affected by the SIP. 42 U.S.C. § 7410(a)(2).

(iii) *Nonattainment Areas*. The CAAA of 1990 addressed the problem that the states still had many areas which had not attained the NAAQS for emissions of one or more pollutants. Some states lacked clearly defined programs to make progress toward compliance. The CAAA of 1990 amended the CAA to require that SIPs provide for annual incremental reductions of emissions of nonattainment pollutants and the EPA may order further reductions to attain compliance by the required date. To measure progress, SIPs must provide for current inventories of nonattainment pollutants, identify and quantify emissions from new permitted sources, and contain measures that will automatically be implemented if there is a failure to make reasonable progress or to attain compliance by the required date. 42 U.S.C. § 7501 *et seq.*

The CAAA of 1990 extended the deadline dates for compliance with the NAAQS. However, in addition to the general steps already described, it also amended the CAA to impose specific requirements applicable to existing sources and new or modified sources and to particular pollutants. SIPs must require that all existing major stationary sources in nonattainment areas implement reasonably available control technology (RACT). SIPs must also require that permits be obtained for construction and operation of all new or modified major stationary sources in nonattainment areas and that the grant of such permits be subject to strict nonattainment new source review requirements. 42 U.S.C. § 7502 *et seq.*

For areas that have not attained the NAAQS, the CAAA of 1990 requires that each SIP contain additional requirements applicable to nitrogen oxides, volatile organic compounds, carbon monoxide, particulate matter (PM-10), sulfur oxides, nitrogen dioxide and lead. 42 U.S.C. §§ 7511 to 7514a. For example, ozone nonattainment areas are divided into five categories: marginal, moderate, serious, severe and extreme with design values and compliance deadlines for each ranging from 3 to 20 years. Depending on the degree of ozone nonattainment, increasingly strict control programs must be imposed on existing and stationary sources of ozone precursors, i.e., volatile organic compounds and nitrogen oxides. In ozone nonattainment areas, the states must also implement new or stricter programs such as vehicle inspection and maintenance, transportation controls and clean fuels or advanced control technology systems.

(iv) *Prevention of Significant Deterioration.* The CAAA of 1990 extended PSD requirements applicable to areas that are in compliance with the NAAQS. The CAA divides the areas into three classes. Class I includes parks and wilderness areas where only the smallest increases of air pollution are allowed. Other areas are considered Class II, unless redesignated, and must meet primary and secondary NAAQS and additional limits on increases of particulate matter and sulfur dioxide. The initial increments and ceilings are prescribed in the CAA and the USEPA is required to adopt regulations applying PSD restrictions to additional pollutants. By following specified procedures, states can redesignate areas as Class III which has more lenient limits for pollutant emission increases. No "major emitting facility" may be constructed in any area to which the PSD requirements apply without a permit, which may be issued only after demonstration that emissions from the facility will meet specified requirements including control of each emitted pollutant by the best available control technology (BACT). 42 U.S.C. § 7470 *et seq.*

The PSD requirements also include a program to prevent future, and to remedy existing, impairment of visibility in Class I federal areas. Visibility is a factor which must be considered before a construction permit can be issued for a new or modified major stationary source. In addition, certain existing sources can be required to install and operate best available retrofit technology (BART). 42 U.S.C. § 7491 *et seq.*

C.   New Source Performance Standards

The USEPA has adopted new source performance standards (NSPS) for 61 categories of industrial plants (such as cement and glass plants) and equipment (such as incinerators and stationary gas turbines). New plants and equipment in these categories must meet technology based standards which require the best system of emission reduction adequately demonstrated (BADT), taking into account cost and other factors. The NSPS typically apply mass emission limits to quantities of pollutants emitted by a plant or equipment and also apply opacity (visible emission) limits. If an existing plant or equipment is reconstructed or modified, it is treated as a new source and must comply with NSPS. Compliance with NSPS must be demonstrated by monitoring, reporting and record-keeping. 42 U.S.C. § 7411; 40 C.F.R. Part 60.

Throughout the U.S., companies operating facilities in existence prior to the dates requiring compliance with NSPS are careful to limit changes to steps which will not be a modification or renovation requiring the major costs required to meet NSPS. If they go too far, a state agency or the USEPA may contend that a new permit is required containing NSPS limits. Companies have sometimes successfully challenged a decision by an environmental agency to require a permit for the installation of replacement facilities or equipment. *Celebrezze v. National Lime*, No. 92-989, 38 ERC 1620, 1994 Ohio LEXIS 372 (S. Ct. 3/2/94); *Allstead Inc. v. EPA*, No. 94-3179, 1994 U.S. App. LEXIS 12385 (6th Cir., 3/26/94).

D. National Emission Standards for Hazardous Air Pollutants (NESHAPs)

(i) *Pre-1990 NESHAPs.* Prior to 1990, the USEPA adopted NESHAPs for several pollutants which it found may cause or contribute to air pollution reasonably anticipated to result in mortality or increase in serious irreversible, or incapacitating reversible, illness. They were beryllium, mercury, vinyl chloride, radionuclides from specified sources, benzene from specified sources, asbestos, inorganic arsenic from specified sources, and Radon-222 from uranium mill tailings. A NESHAP was also adopted to cover equipment leaks (fugitive emissions) of a lengthy list of hazardous air pollutants from manufacturing equipment. When the USEPA found that it was not feasible to adopt an emission standard, it could adopt a NESHAP prescribing operating standards as it did in the NESHAP for asbestos. Both new and existing sources were required to comply with NESHAPs, although existing sources could seek exemptions and time extensions. 42 U.S.C. § 7412; 40 C.F.R. Part 61.

(ii) *Post-1990 NESHAPs*. The CAAA of 1990 required the USEPA to adopt standards limiting emissions of hazardous air pollutants from new and existing major sources and also from smaller sources, called "area sources," such as paint shops and dry cleaning stores. The CAAA of 1990 included a minimum list of 189 hazardous air pollutants (HAPs). The USEPA may add or delete chemicals from this list and private parties may petition the USEPA to make additions or deletions. 42 U.S.C. § 7412. The USEPA was also required to issue a list of major sources and area sources of the listed HAPs. The USEPA published the required list at 57 Fed. Reg. 31,576 (7/16/92).

(iii) *Major Sources*. Major sources are those emitting 10 tons per year of any one of the listed HAPs or 25 tons per year of any combination of them. The USEPA published its final schedule for promulgating NESHAPs for toxic air pollutants based on maximum available control technology (MACT) standards on November 16, 1993. Among the most significant actions taken by the USEPA was its issuance of the Hazardous Organic NESHAP, or the HON, at 59 Fed. Reg. 19,402 (4/22/94) requiring the synthetic organic chemical industry and certain other chemical processors operating major sources to apply MACT to reduce emissions (including leaks) of 112 of the 189 HAPs listed in the CAAA of 1990. 40 C.F.R. Part 63, § 63.100 *et seq.* Another action with widespread effect was the USEPA's issuance of a final NESHAP regulating emissions of several HAPs by halogenated solvent cleaners. 59 C.F.R. 61,801 (12/2/94), 40 C.F.R. § 63.460 *et seq.* The USEPA has also issued a final rule providing guidance for state programs regulating HAPs. 58 Fed. Reg. 62,262 (11/26/93).

(iv) *Area Sources.* Area sources are any sources of HAPs in the source categories designated by the USEPA other than a major source. Before 1990, area sources were not subjected to a comprehensive system of federal regulation. They include many small businesses as well as many sources whose emissions are small, although their cumulative effect may be important in some areas. Accordingly, the CAAA of 1990 required that the USEPA list only those categories or subcategories of area sources that it finds present a threat of adverse effects to human health or the environment, individually or in the aggregate. However, the USEPA must list within 5 years sufficient categories or subcategories of area sources to ensure that area sources representing 90% of the area source emissions of the 30 hazardous air pollutants that present the greatest threat to public health in the largest number of urban areas are subject to regulations. Such regulations must be adopted within 10 years. 42 U.S.C. § 7412. An important action to control area source emissions was taken by the USEPA in its Perchloroethylene Dry Cleaning Facilities NESHAP at 58 Fed. Reg. 49,354 (9/22/93) in which area sources are regulated, but less strictly than major sources. 40 C.F.R. § 63.320 *et seq.*

(v) *Technology-Based Standards for NESHAPS.* For new sources, the EPA must establish technology-based standards not less stringent than the emission control level achieved in practice by the best controlled similar source. If an existing source is modified, the modified facility must meet the standards for a new source.

For existing sources, the USEPA must adopt technology- based standards requiring use of maximum available control technology (MACT), which may be less stringent than standards for new sources in the same category but shall not be less stringent, and may be more stringent than (A) the average emission limitations achieved by the best 12% of the existing sources *excluding* certain sources that have within specified recent time periods first achieved compliance with the lowest achievable emission rate (LAER), or (B) the average emission limitation achieved by the best performing five sources in any category with fewer than 30 sources. In its interpretation of the CAAA of 1990, the USEPA has at least initially chosen a strict (or "higher flow") standard for MACT. See 59 Fed. Reg. 29,196 (6/16/94).

The CAAA of 1990 required the USEPA to issue MACT standards for at least 40 source categories within two years after its enactment. All other source categories will be controlled according to a schedule to be met within 10 years after enactment. Owners and operators must comply with a new MACT standard within 3 years after its effective date. Extensions for achieving compliance will be available to companies making significant improvements which do not fully achieve the MACT standards.

However, qualifying facilities which achieve a 90% reduction of certain HAPs may be entitled to defer compliance with the MACT standards for six years. 57 Fed. Reg. 61,970 (12/29/92) codified at 40 C.F.R. § 63.70 *et seq.*

(vi) *Health-Based Standards for NESHAPs.* In addition to the MACT standards, the CAAA of 1990 provides that the USEPA must develop health-based standards unless Congress acts to defer or delete that requirement. The health standards applicable to pollutants classified as known, probable or possible human carcinogens will be designed to reduce lifetime excess cancer risk to the individual most exposed to less than one in one million.

(vii) *Accidental Releases.* A program for the prevention or mitigation of accidental releases of regulated substances and any other extremely hazardous substance is established by the CAAA of 1990. A general duty was imposed on owners and operators of stationary sources producing, processing, handling or storing such substances to identify hazards which may result from accidental releases, to design and maintain a safe facility so as to prevent such releases, and to minimize the consequences for such releases as do occur. The USEPA was required to issue regulations requiring that owners and operators of stationary sources adopt and register with the USEPA a risk management plan (RMP). The USEPA was also required to issue within 24 months an initial list of at least 100 substances which pose the greatest risk of causing death, injury or serious adverse effects to human health or the environment from accidental releases. A Chemical Safety and Hazard Investigation Board was created with broad investigative and other powers relating to accidental releases. 42 U.S.C. § 7412(r).

The USEPA proposed a rule governing RMPs in 58 Fed. Reg. 54, 190, 10/20/93, but it encountered widespread opposition because it would have required hazard assessments of worst-case scenarios based on unrealistic assumptions. Thus, this rule has not yet been adopted. The USEPA has issued the initial list of regulated substances including 77 toxic substances, 63 flammable substances, and certain explosives defined by the U.S. Department of Transportation as those that have an explosion hazard. 59 Fed. Reg. 4,478 (1/31/94); 40 C.F.R. Part 68. The USEPA has proposed rules providing guidance for state accidental release programs at 58 Fed. Reg. 29,296 (5/19/93). The CAAA of 1990 contemplates that the USEPA's rules will be coordinated with the chemical process safety management standard of the Occupational Safety and Health Administration (OSHA) described later. 29 C.F.R. § 1910.119.

Responding to the extensive public comments, the USEPA published a supplemental notice of proposed rulemaking. 60 Fed. Reg. 13,526 (3/13/95). In the supplemental notice, the USEPA revised its assumptions for worst case scenarios to make them somewhat more realistic and proposed three tiers for RMPs. A Tier 1 source would prepare a brief RMP demonstrating and certifying that its worst case release would not reach any public or environmental receptors of concern. A Tier 2 source would conduct an offsite consequence analysis, document a 5-year accident history, implement prevention steps, prepare an emergency response plan, and submit an RMP, but need not take steps to comply with the prevention and emergency response programs. A Tier 3 source would be required to develop and implement the full risk management program.

(viii) *Court Review of HAP Listing.* The courts may nullify a listing of a substance as a HAP if the EPA's methods in reaching its decision are found to be arbitrary. For example, its listing of methylene diphenyl diisocyanate (MDI) was nullified in *Chemical Manufacturers Association v. EPA*, 28 F.3d 1259 (D.C. Cir. 1994).

E.   Motor Vehicles and Clean Fuels

The CAAA of 1990 imposed stricter controls on vehicles, fuels and fuel additives. Stricter tailpipe emission standards were imposed on automobiles and trucks. Leaded gasoline cannot be sold for motor vehicle use after December 31, 1995. Unleaded fuels must be generally used thereafter. In ozone nonattainment areas, reformulated gasoline with 2.0% oxygen content, lower aromatic content and other characteristics must be used. In carbon monoxide nonattainment areas, oxygenated gasoline with 2.7% oxygen content and other specified characteristics was required. Fleet vehicles and the fuels used in fleet vehicles in nonattainment areas were subjected to special restrictions.

The CAAA of 1990 further restricted the introduction of new fuel additives and required that the sulfur content of diesel fuel be reduced. It also modified the mandatory warranties that vehicle manufacturers must provide for emission control components. States were authorized to adopt some regulatory standards, but they must correspond to California programs. Other provisions included programs for urban buses and nonroad vehicles and engines. 42 U.S.C. § 7507 and §§ 7581-7590.

The USEPA's regulations on fuels and fuel additives are contained in 40 C.F.R. Parts 79 and 80. The regulations on motor vehicles and motor vehicle engines are at 40 C.F.R. Parts 85 and 86. The regulations on aircraft and aircraft engines are at 40 C.F.R. Part 87. The clean fuel vehicles regulations are at 40 C.F.R. Part 88 (57 Fed. Reg. 60,046 (12/17/92) and 58 Fed. Reg. 11,901 (3/1/93)). The fuel economy labelling and fuel economy retrofit device regulations are at 40 C.F.R. Parts 600 and 610.

F.   Acid Deposition Control (Acid Rain)

The CAAA of 1990 established programs to control and reduce emissions of sulfur oxides and nitrogen oxides from electric utilities that are believed to create "acid rain" damaging forests and lakes. The programs consist of a complex package of permit requirements and emission allowances that can be used for new or modified sources or can be transferred. The sulfur dioxide limitations will be implemented in two phases.

The Phase I provisions require that, after January 1, 1995, 111 electric utility plants located primarily in the Midwestern United States must reduce sulfur dioxide emissions to 2.5 pounds per million BTU multiplied by their average 1985-87 fuel consumption. However, a reserve of bonus allowances administered by the USEPA to provide flexibility during this first phase are provided as well as numerous exceptions. Plants that elect to repower their facilities using qualifying clean coal technologies can obtain extended compliance dates and extra allowances for reducing sulfur dioxide emissions below 1.2 pounds per million BTU.

The Phase II provisions require that, after January 1, 2000, all steam-electric utilities must reduce SO_2 emissions below 1.2 pounds per million BTU. Again, a system of allowances and other requirements and exceptions is provided. Title IV contains provisions authorizing matching grants up to $2.5 billion for the development of clean coal technology processes and equipment. 42 U.S.C. § 7651.

The USEPA published its final rule on auctions, direct sales, and independent power producer guarantees under the sulfur dioxide emission reduction program at 56 Fed. Reg. 65,592 (12/17/91). In adopting the rule, the USEPA briefly discussed the announcement by the Chicago Board of Trade on July 17, 1991 to create a futures market for sulfur dioxide allowances. 40 C.F.R. Part 73, Subparts A and E. The USEPA published its final core rules for the Acid Rain Program at 58 Fed. Reg. 3,590 (1/11/93). These rules cover general provisions and permits, the allowance system, continuous emissions monitoring, excess emissions, reserves, permits and administrative appeals. 40 C.F.R. Parts 72 to 78.

Compliance by electric utilities with the acid deposition control regulations creates difficult choices whether and how to use high or low sulfur coal, oil or nuclear fuels and whether to incur the cost of capital equipment to control emissions. These choices have been made even more difficult in recent years by government-mandated programs requiring utilities to purchase power from cogeneration plants and to "wheel" power through their lines and facilities for the benefit of customers who wish to purchase power from distant sources.

G.   Stratospheric Ozone Provisions

The CAAA of 1990 added provisions to the CAA to restrict chemical substances believed by environmental advocates to deplete stratospheric ozone. The amendments imposed a freeze and require eventual elimination of these substances in cooperation with the Montreal Protocol. Class I chemicals include chlorofluorocarbons (CFCs), halons, carbon tetrachloride and methyl chloroform. They must be phased out by the year 2000. Class II chemicals consist of hydrochlorofluorocarbons (HCFCs). They will be phased out by 2030. Other requirements include monitoring and reporting, recycling and disposal, standards for servicing motor vehicle air conditioners and labelling. The USEPA was directed to adopt regulations within two years governing replacement chemicals and processes and may recommend research programs to promote their development and sale. The USEPA was required to publish a list of safe and unsafe substitutes for Class I and II chemicals and to ban the use of unsafe substitutes.

The USEPA has adopted regulations designed to implement the CAAA of 1990 restrictions on "ozone-depleting substances" at 40 C.F.R. Part 82. They include production and consumption controls including baseline allowances and allocations (57 Fed. Reg. 33,754 (7/30/92)); servicing of motor vehicle air conditioners (57 Fed. Reg. 31,242 (7/14/92)); a ban on nonessential products containing Class I substances (58 Fed. Reg. 4,768 (1/15/93)); labelling (57 Fed. Reg. 19,166 (5/4/93); 58 Fed. Reg. 8,136 (2/11/93)), and recycling of controlled substances (58 Fed. Reg. 28,660 (5/14/93)). The USEPA adopted a Significant New Alternatives Policy (SNAP) under which it published a list of acceptable substitutes for ozone-depleting substances. 59 Fed. Reg. 13044, 3/18/94. See also the lists published in 59 Fed. Reg. 44240, 8/26/94 and 60 Fed. Reg. 3318,

1/13/95 and 40 C.F.R. Part 82. The USEPA also issued a notice of proposed rulemaking restricting the use of some substitutes. 59 Fed. Reg. 49108 (9/26/94).

In general, industry has moved rapidly to comply with the new laws and regulations and to develop substitute products. However, the adequacy of substitute products has not so far been fully demonstrated to the public. Thus, the press has recently reported the growth of "black markets" for CFCs. That will be an enforcement problem for the USEPA.

H.   Permits

Title V of the Clean Air Act Amendments of 1990 established a new permit program for the CAA, using experience developed in administering the national pollutant discharge elimination system under the Clean Water Act. The USEPA issued the final operating permit rule on establishing minimum elements for state and local programs. 57 Fed. Reg. 32,250 (7/21/92) codified at 40 C.F.R. Part 70. After the effective date of each program, it is a violation of the CAA for any person to operate a major source, an area source or other source required to have a permit except in compliance with a permit issued by a permitting authority under the applicable program.

The minimum elements of each state program must include: (1) adoption of forms and procedures for applications; (2) establishing procedures and forms for monitoring and reporting; (3) annual or other fees sufficient to cover allreasonable costs required to develop and implement the program; (4) adequate personnel and funding; (5) adequate authority for the permitting agency to issue permits for a fixed term not to exceed five years incorporating emission limits and other requirements, to enforce the permits and to terminate, modify or revoke and reissue them for cause; (6) assurance that no permit will be issued if the USEPA objects in a timely manner; (7) permit processing procedures including public notice opportunity and for public comment and hearings; (8) provisions authorizing judicial review in the event of unreasonable delay; (9) procedures to afford public access to permit files; (10) requirements that major source permits with a term of three or more years be subject to revision to incorporate standards and regulations adopted after their issuance; and (11) provisions allowing changes within a permitted facility without requiring a permit revision if the changes are not modifications and do not exceed the emissions allowed by the permit.

The fees charged to obtain and maintain permits must cover direct and indirect costs for activities such as permit reviews; monitoring; preparing generally applicable regulations; modelling, analysis and demonstrations; preparing inventories; and tracking emissions. Thus, the cost of the programs will be borne by the owners and operators of regulated sources. Failure to pay fees is subject to a 50% penalty plus interest.

Permit applications must be submitted with a compliance plan and schedule including progress reports no less often than six months until compliance is achieved. Permitting authorities are required to approve or disapprove a permit application within 18 months. Each permit must contain conditions including enforceable emission limits and standards, a compliance schedule, and periodic submission of any required monitoring reports. Each permit must also contain inspection, entry, monitoring, compliance certification, and reporting requirements. Permit holders must be required to certify compliance no less often than annually and to promptly report any deviations from permit requirements.

Permitting authorities must provide to the USEPA a copy of each permit application and compliance plan and each proposed and final permit. If any permit contains provisions not in compliance with the CAA, the USEPA is required to object to its issuance and state its reasons. If the USEPA objects, the permitting authority may not issue the permit unless it is revised to meet the objection.

Permitting authorities must also notify all states (A) whose air quality may be affected and that are contiguous to the state in which an emission originates, *or* (B) that are within 50 miles of the source. They must provide an opportunity for these states to submit written recommendations.

19

I.   Enforcement

Prior to the CAAA of 1990, the USEPA already had extensive enforcement powers -- far beyond those of other government agencies with responsibility for programs vital to the public. However, the CAAA of 1990 further expanded the powers of the USEPA in the administration and enforcement of the CAA.

The CAAA of 1990 authorizes and directs the USEPA to take direct action to enforce SIP, permit, new source and other requirements if it finds that a state has failed to take enforcement action. In addition to civil and criminal actions, the USEPA can directly impose compliance actions such as monitoring, sampling, certifications, record keeping and reporting. Criminal penalties for knowing violations are increased from misdemeanors to felonies and new criminal and civil actions have been added. Monetary fines may be imposed up to $250,000 per violation for individuals and $500,000 per violation for corporations as well as imprisonment for terms up to 15 years. Fines for continuing violations may be imposed daily.

Liability of corporate employees is generally limited to senior management personnel and officers and, except for knowing and willful violations, does not include stationary engineers, technicians and other such employees who are carrying out normal activities and acting under orders from the employer. Revised citizen suit provisions allow citizens to seek penalties to be deposited in a U.S. Treasury fund for use by the USEPA in compliance and enforcement activities. The USEPA may also pay awards up to $10,000 to "whistleblowers" who furnish information or services leading to a conviction or penalty.

The Joint Explanatory Statement of the Senate/House Conference Committee contains several interesting statements about the enforcement provisions. First, the criminal sanctions for recordkeeping, filing and other omissions are not intended to penalize inadvertent errors. Second, the criminal penalties are not intended to discourage owners or operators from conducting self-evaluations or self-audits and acting to correct any problems identified. On the contrary, they are to be encouraged. The criminal penalties should not be applied to persons acting in good faith who promptly report the results of an audit and act to correct any deviation. Knowledge gained solely in these activities should not ordinarily form the basis of the intent that results in a finding of criminal activities.

V. CLEAN WATER ACT

A.   General

The Clean Water Act (CWA), 33 U.S.C. § 1251 *et seq.*, was adopted to protect fish, shellfish and wildlife, restore water recreation, and eliminate discharge of pollutants into U.S. waters. The CWA provides several programs: (1) technology based national effluent standards by industry; (2) water quality standards; (3) a permit program restricting discharges from point sources known as the national pollutant discharge elimination system (NPDES); (4) proposed regulation of nonpoint source effluent discharges such as surface water runoff from industrial plant sites; (5) stormwater permit programs; (6) a spill control program; (7) permit programs for dredging and filling in tidal and freshwater wetlands; and (8) construction grants for publicly owned treatment works (POTWs).

B.   Effluent Standards

The USEPA's Effluent Guidelines and Standards are published in 40 C.F.R. Parts 400 to 471. They distinguish between sources discharging directly into waters and those discharging to POTWs. They also distinguish between existing sources and new sources. An existing source which is substantially modified is treated as a new source.

Existing direct discharge sources were originally required to apply best practicable control technology (BPT). Since July 1, 1983, they must apply best available technology economically feasible (BAT). However, a separate and relatively lenient standard of best conventional technology (BCT) applies to conventional pollutants: biological oxygen demand (BOD), suspended solids (SS), fecal coliform bacteria, pH, and oil and grease. A separate standard also applies to nonconventional, nontoxic pollutants which includes limits applicable to ammonia, chlorine, color and iron.

Section 306 of the CWA, 33 U.S.C. § 1316, requires that new direct discharge sources must apply the best available demonstrated control technology. In developing new source performance standards (NSPS), the USEPA must consider not only discharge controls but other controls achieved by process and operating methods. The USEPA is not specifically directed to consider economic and technological factors. Issuance of a permit for a major new source may require an EIS under NEPA. 40 C.F.R. Part 6, Subpart F.

Section 307(b) of the CWA, 33 U.S.C. § 1317, requires that industrial facilities discharging to a POTW must pretreat their effluent. The regulations provide general standards (40 C.F.R. Part 403) to protect POTW operations and categorical standards (40 C.F.R. Part 405 *et seq.*) applicable to specific industries. The general standards prohibit discharge of pollutants which may cause fire, explosion, corrosion, obstructions, excessive heat or other conditions upsetting treatment at a POTW. The categorical standards apply to incompatible pollutants which a POTW is not designed to treat. Industrial facilities must pretreat incompatible pollutants in a manner equivalent to the BAT or NSPS standards applicable to direct dischargers, i.e., they must comply with pretreatment standards for new sources (PSNS) or pretreatment standards for existing sources (PSES). If a POTW has an approved pretreatment program for incompatible pollutants, it can charge user fees for its pretreatment capability and can grant removal credits to dischargers for their pretreatment operations. An attempt by environmentalists to block the grant of removal credits by POTWs was rejected in *Sierra Club v. EPA*, 992 F.2d 337 (D.C. Cir. 1993).

In July 1990, the USEPA published amendments to its regulations to impose greater regulatory obligations upon POTWs to prevent discharges of pollutants from passing untreated through their facilities or interfering with their operations. The amended regulations required POTWs with approved pretreatment plans to issue permits or to establish equivalent control mechanisms for each industrial user. 55 Fed. Reg. 30,082 (7/24/90) codified at 40 C.F.R. Part 403.

The amended regulations prohibited some discharges directly and left others to be regulated by each POTW. Discharge of ignitable, reactive and other pollutants which may create a fire or explosion hazard in a POTW is prohibited, including those with a flashpoint of less than 140° F (60°C) as determined by closed cup testers in accordance with specified ASTM methods. Discharge of pollutants which result in toxic gases, vapors or fumes within a POTW in a quantity that may cause acute worker health and safety problems is prohibited. Discharge of petroleum oil, nonbiodegradable cutting oil, or products of mineral oil origin in amounts that would cause interference or pass through at the POTW is prohibited. Discharge of trucked or hauled wastes, except at specific discharge points designated by a POTW, is prohibited.

The regulations impose reporting requirements on significant industrial users, i.e., those that discharge 25,000 gallons per day of process wastewater to a POTW excluding sanitary, noncontact cooling and boiler blowdown waters. Each industrial user must notify the POTW, the USEPA Regional Waste Management Division Director and state hazardous waste authorities in writing of any discharge to a POTW of a substance considered a hazardous waste under the Resource Conservation and Recovery Act (RCRA). Industrial users are required to file semiannual reports of effluent monitoring data including a description of the concentration and flow of pollutants to the POTW. All industrial users must also notify the POTW in advance of any substantial change in the volume or character of pollutants in their discharge. Sampling and analysis may be performed by the POTW in lieu of the industrial user.

POTWs with approved pretreatment programs are required to conduct at least one inspection and sampling visit annually for each significant industrial user. They must also evaluate whether each significant industrial user needs a plan to control slug discharges, i.e., accidental spills or nonroutine batch discharges. The regulations impose testing requirements and restrictions on POTWs that are likely to compel them to adopt strict future local regulations governing industrial discharges. For example, POTWs with a design influent flow equal to or greater than one million gallons per day and any POTW having (or required to have) an approved pretreatment program must submit the results of a whole effluent biological toxicity test to the USEPA as part of its NPDES permit application. The regulations also create specific numeric limits for certain toxic pollutants in sewage sludge, specify acceptable sludge management practices and encourage the development of local limits to keep pollutants out of sludge which interfere with its proper disposal.

The USEPA published a plan for developing new and revised effluent guidelines at 57 Fed. Reg. 41,000 (9/8/92).

C.   Water Quality Standards

Section 301 of the CWA, 33 U.S.C. § 1311, requires that the states adopt water quality standards for waters within their jurisdiction in accordance with USEPA regulations at 40 C.F.R. Part 131. These standards must regulate conventional pollutants, nonconventional nontoxic pollutants and toxic pollutants consisting primarily of the 65 "priority pollutant" categories listed in a court order against the USEPA obtained in 1976 by the Natural Resources Defense Council (NRDC), a private environmental advocacy organization, and now listed at 40 C.F.R. § 401.15. In order to meet water quality standards, the CWA authorizes states to impose effluent limits stricter than the BAT and NSPS standards. 33 U.S.C. § 1312. The industrial states have been reluctant to exceed federal mandates for areas such as the Houston Ship Channel. However, Section 304(1) added to the CWA in 1987 required the states to inventory and report waters where technology-based limits were not achieving water quality standards for toxic pollutants.

D.   NPDES Program and Permits

The CWA program having the most direct impact on industry is the NPDES permit program. The CWA prohibits all discharges of pollutants from point sources into navigable waters unless allowed by an NPDES permit. The term "pollutant" includes chemical, biological and other industrial substances as well as sewage, solid waste and dredging spoils. A point source is a means of conveyance such as a pipe, ditch, conduit or vessel, but also may include surface runoff from land. Navigable waters include coastal waters, lakes, rivers and their tributaries such as non-navigable creeks and streams. The USEPA regulations governing the NPDES program are at 40 C.F.R. Parts 121-125. A great majority of the states have adopted programs approved by the USEPA so that their state environmental agencies can grant permits and administer the programs. NPDES and corresponding state permits set limits based on USEPA standards for toxic pollutants and water quality (40 C.F.R. Parts 129-131) and for effluents from particular industrial processes (40 C.F.R. Parts 401-471). USEPA's guidelines for test procedures are at 40 C.F.R. Part 136.

Permit applications are a lengthy and detailed effort, especially for a new source where the application must be accompanied by a new source questionnaire containing detailed manufacturing process data. Several government agencies, private environmental organizations, the media and the public may become involved. Each permit requires periodic or continuous monitoring, record keeping and reporting including any violations. Over the years, permit standards have become stricter. In recent years, bioassay requirements have been added to permits requiring demonstration that small marine organisms (such as flathead minnows or mysid shrimp) can live in diluted samples of the effluent.

E.   Nonpointsource Effluent

Much of the pollution discharged to the nation's waters comes from surface runoff and other nonpoint sources. Major nonpoint sources include farms and municipalities which cannot readily be regulated like private industry. The CWA requires the states to provide inventories and reports on compliance with water quality standards showing failure to attain compliance traceable to nonpoint source discharges of toxic pollutants. The CWA also provides funding for state studies of nonpoint source controls.

In its definition of a point source, the CWA excludes agriculturally and silviculturally related nonpoint sources of pollution, including runoff from manure disposal areas and from land used for livestock and crop production. However, it includes a concentrated animal feeding operation. Environmental groups oppose this agricultural exclusion. Recently, an environmental group and the USEPA persuaded a federal appellate court that a large dairy farm should be treated as a concentrated animal feeding operation and that its entire operation was a point source subject to regulation under the CWA. *Concerned Residents v. Southview Farm*, 34 F.3d 114 (2nd Cir. 1994).

F. Stormwater

The CWA regulates stormwater discharges from industrial activities and larger municipalities. Stormwater permit regulations were adopted in 1990 applicable to large and medium-sized cities, some counties and certain industries. 55 Fed. Reg. 47,990 (11/16/90). The final rule establishing general permit requirements and reporting requirements for stormwater discharges associated with industrial activity was published in April, 1992. 57 Fed. Reg. 11,394 (4/2/92). In general, existing industrial facilities were required to apply for a permit by October 1, 1992 and the permit issuance deadline was October 1, 1993. Federal and state regulations allow some facilities to be covered by general or group permits rather than requiring industrial facility permits. For example, see the draft multisector permit proposed by the USEPA at 58 Fed. Reg. 61,146 (11/19/93). Pollution control methods required by stormwater permits include finding and removing illegal sewer connections, halting dumping in sewers and preventing spills. State environmental agencies may impose "best management practices" rather than numerical limits in appropriate situations.

Stormwater regulatory programs have encountered lengthy delays, partially because of a successful challenge of the USEPA's regulations in *Natural Resources Defense Council v. EPA*, 966 F.2d 1292 (9th Cir. 1992). Among other things, The NRDC objected to exemptions for light industry and small construction sites.

G. Spills

The CWA prohibits and requires notification to federal and state agencies of discharges of oil or hazardous substances not in compliance with an existing or pending NPDES permit if they equal or exceed reportable quantities listed at 40 C.F.R. Parts 116 and 117. Spill control plans are also required. In addition to fines and penalties, the discharger is liable for cleanup costs for spills of oil and hazardous substances. 33 U.S.C. § 1321.

H.   Wetlands

The CWA regulates dredging and filling in tidal and fresh water wetlands. Wetlands are areas inundated or saturated by groundwater and normally supporting vegetation typically adapted for life in saturated soil conditions, i.e., swamps, marshes, bogs and the like. Prior to dredging or filling, a permit must be obtained from the U.S. Army Corps of Engineers and any state agency having similar jurisdiction. Normal farming, agriculture and ranching and certain maintenance and construction activities are exempt. 33 U.S.C. § 1344. See, however, *U.S. v. Brace*, No. 94-3076, 1994 U.S. App. LEXIS 32986 (3d Cir. Nov. 22, 1994).

A permit application must describe in detail not only the dredging and filling activities, but also related construction projects such as buildings, bridges and docks. The Corps of Engineers must notify other interested government agencies and the public. It must also determine whether an environmental impact statement is required under NEPA. The Corps of Engineers considers the public interest, effects on wetlands and adjacent waters, wildlife resources, water quality and other factors in deciding whether to grant a permit. 33 C.F.R. § 320.4. Permits can be challenged in a U.S. District Court which is limited to determining whether the permit decision was arbitrary or abusive.

I.   Sewage Sludge

The USEPA's regulations governing sewage sludge are contained in 40 C.F.R. Parts 501 *et seq*. Part 501 sets forth the USEPA's procedures for approval of state sludge management programs. In 1993, the USEPA published Part 503 setting national standards for use and disposal of sewage sludge including standards for certain metals and pathogens in sewage sludge. However, portions of the

Part 503 regulations were remanded in *Leather Industries v. EPA*, 40 F.3d 392 (D.C. Cir. 1994).

VI.   RESOURCE CONSERVATION AND RECOVERY ACT

A.   General

The Resource Conservation and Recovery Act (RCRA), 42 U.S.C. § 6901 *et seq.*, governs the generation, storage, transportation treatment and disposal of solid waste including hazardous waste. Under RCRA, the USEPA has adopted regulations establishing a Hazardous Waste Management System which applies throughout the United States. 40 C.F.R. Part 260 *et seq.* The System establishes permit requirements for hazardous waste related activities and the use of a "cradle to the grave" manifest system which accounts for hazardous waste from the generator's facility to final disposal.

B.   Solid Waste

For a material to be subject to RCRA, it must be a "solid waste". Solid waste is broadly defined to include any garbage, refuse, certain sludges and any other discarded material including solid, liquid, semisolid or contained gaseous materials. However, the definition excludes a few wastes such as domestic sewage, effluent discharges allowed by NPDES permits, irrigation flows, some nuclear materials, some mining residues, and some recyclable wastes. 42 U.S.C. § 6903(27) and 40 C.F.R. §§ 261.2 and 261.4(a).

RCRA delegates the management of nonhazardous solid wastes primarily to the states which are required to ban "open dumping" and adopt solid waste management plans implemented by laws and regulations. The role of the USEPA is to establish minimum criteria and to approve state plans. 40 C.F.R. Parts 240 to 258. See *Sierra Club v. USEPA*, 992 F.2d 337 (D.C. Cir. 1993).

Some states, such as Illinois and New Jersey, have adopted elaborate solid waste management laws and regulations designed to control all aspects of solid waste including generation, collection, transportation, disposal, recycling, reclamation and beneficial reuse. They have created district waste flow laws and rules under which franchise monopolies are granted and prohibitions, restrictions and charges are imposed on the movement into and out of the state or the districts. The restrictive "waste flow" laws of some states have been held in violation of the U.S. Constitution because of their discriminatory effect on interstate commerce. *City of Philadelphia v. New Jersey*, 437 U.S. 617 (1978); *Chemical Waste Management, Inc. v. Hunt*, 119 L.Ed.2d 121, (1992); *Fort Gratiot Sanitary Landfill, Inc. v. Michigan Department of Natural Resources*, 112 S.Ct. 2019, 34 ERC 1721 (1992); *Chemical Waste Management v. Templet*, 967 F.2d 1058, (5th Cir. 1992), cert. den. 61 USLW 3498 (1993); *Government Suppliers Consolidating Services v. Bayh*, 975 F.2d 1267 (7th Cir. 1992). *See also Clarkstown v. C&A Carbone, Inc.*, 182 A.D.2d 213, (N.Y. Sup. Ct. 1992), appeal denied 80 N.Y.2d 760 (1992); cert. granted 61 USLW 3787 (1993); affirmed 114 S.Ct. 1677 (1994)

C.   Hazardous Waste

Hazardous waste is solid waste which either (1) appears on any of the hazardous waste lists adopted by the USEPA in 40 C.F.R. Part 261 and includes series designated as F, K, P and U or (2) has specific characteristics of ignitability, corrosivity, reactivity or toxicity measured by a toxicity characteristic leaching procedure (TCLP). However, exceptions for certain solid wastes are provided in 40 C.F.R. § 261.4(b).

The listed hazardous wastes are fairly easy to identify. The "F" series consists of wastes from non-specific sources such as spent solvents. The "K" series consists of wastes from specific sources such as wood preservative bottom sediment sludges that use creosote and/or pentachlorophenol. The "P" series consists of a lengthy list of commercial chemical products and intermediates which are acute hazardous wastes if and when discarded or used in other ways that amount to disposal. The "U" series consists of other toxic chemicals. 40 C.F.R. § 261.31 *et seq.*

"Characteristic" wastes are not so easy to identify. The identification depends on the results of tests for the applicable characteristics. For example, wastes containing many common paints, solvents and adhesives may be hazardous because they are ignitable, i.e., flashpoint less than 140° F as measured by the regulatory tests. Waste may be corrosive, i.e., pH less than 2.0 or higher than 12.5. Waste containing peroxide residues may be reactive. Wastes containing partially soluble heavy metals may be toxic if the tests show they are likely to leach into groundwater.

The USEPA adopted a rule in 1980 that a mixture of listed hazardous waste and a nonhazardous solid waste is considered a hazardous waste unless it meets certain exemption requirements. 40 C.F.R. § 261.3(a)(2). The USEPA also adopted a rule in 1980 that a waste generated from treatment, storage or disposal of hazardous waste is considered a hazardous waste unless it meets exemption requirements. 40 C.F.R. § 261.3(b)(2). These rules were held invalid in *Shell Oil Company v. EPA*, 950 F.2d 741 (D.C. Cir. 1991) on grounds that they had been adopted without sufficient notice and opportunity for comment. Congress then adopted legislation allowing the rules to remain temporarily in effect, but directed the USEPA to readopt the rules by October 1, 1994. The temporary rules were upheld in *Mobil Oil Corp. v. EPA*, No. 92-1211 (D.C. Cir., 9/23/94). The USEPA did not meet the October 31, 1994 deadline, but is expected to issue new rules during 1995.

D.   Recycling, Reclamation and Reuse

The definitions in 40 C.F.R. Part 261 are carefully drafted to encourage, but allow the USEPA to regulate, recycling, reclamation and beneficial reuse activities. The USEPA is aware that thousands of commercial products began as byproducts or coproducts of manufacturing processes producing other products. Industries such as the steel industry depend upon recycling of scrap metal. Industries such as the chemical industry have for decades returned raw materials for multiple passes through catalytic or other production streams to create greater yields. The regulations allow these activities, subject to restrictions. However, materials continue to be solid waste if they are abandoned by disposal, burning or incineration, or certain other activities. Materials also continue to be solid waste if they are recycled but are then land applied, burned or accumulated speculatively. 40 C.F.R. § 261.6.

E.   Generator Responsibilities

Generators of hazardous waste must obtain an identification number from the USEPA. They must identify hazardous waste and must package and label containers and placard vehicles in which they place it. Generators can store hazardous waste for only 90 days without a storage permit. If waste is transported, the generator must prepare a manifest for each shipment which must be signed by all transporters and also by all treatment, storage or disposal (TSD) facilities to which the waste is transferred. Copies of the manifests must be kept and periodic reports submitted. These and other rules (including rules applicable to exports and imports) are contained in 40 C.F.R. Part 262. Small quantity generators (less than 2,200 pounds per month) are subject to somewhat more lenient regulations which allow, for example, six months storage without a storage permit. 40 C.F.R. § 261.5 and § 262.34(d)-(f).

F.   Transporter Responsibilities

Transporters of hazardous waste must obtain an identification number, complete their part of each manifest, make and keep records, file reports and deliver only to facilities having permits. They can store up to 10 days at a transfer facility without a storage permit. A transporter must obtain a signed copy of the manifest from any other transporter to whom waste is delivered or from the operator of the TSD facility. Transporters must report spills of hazardous waste, take any immediate action to protect health and the environment, and clean up the spills. 40 C.F.R. Part 263.

G.   TSD Facilities

Each owner or operator of a TSD facility (including those who are also generators or transporters) must obtain a permit for each facility. TSD facilities in operation on November 19, 1980, when the RCRA regulations of USEPA became effective, were automatically granted interim status permits and required to meet interim standards. These facilities were also required to apply for final permits and can be closed only in compliance with comprehensive closing and post-closing agreements. New TSD facilities must have a final permit before commencing operation. 40 C.F.R. Parts 264-267 and Part 270.

Both the interim and final requirements for TSD permits are extensive and detailed. They include design specifications for treatment facilities, such as biooxidation ponds, and for disposal facilities, such as landfills and incinerators. For example, land disposal facilities must be double-lined and include leachate monitoring and collection systems. Wastes must be analyzed in accordance with specified methods. The regulations require personnel training, inspections and security procedures, alarms and communication equipment, spill plans, record keeping and reporting, groundwater monitoring, insurance, cooperation with community officials, closure plans, and post closure plans including monitoring for at least 30 years. Each TSD facility must provide financial assurance for its closure and post-closure obligations by a surety bond, letter of credit or other sufficient demonstration that adequate funds will be available. 40 C.F.R. Parts 264-267 and Part 270.

Facilities closed prior to November 19, 1980 are not subject to the Hazardous Waste Management System. However, owners and operators of any facility which held an interim status or final permit at any time are responsible for corrective action throughout the entire facility, including contamination occurring prior to November 19, 1980, as well as any offsite areas where contamination has migrated. 42 U.S.C. § 6924(u)-(v); 40 C.F.R. § 264.101. *See also* 58 Fed. Reg. 8,658 (2/16/93). These corrective action obligations have led many owners and operators of old industrial facilities to conduct their businesses so as to carefully refrain (even at much effort and cost) from activities that would require a TSD permit and trigger prohibitively costly corrective actions.

H.   Underground Storage Tanks

RCRA provides a national program regulating underground storage tanks (USTs). The USEPA has adopted comprehensive regulations applicable to USTs containing oil or hazardous substances with a variety of exceptions including some small tanks, tanks containing heating oil used on premises, septic tanks, pipeline facilities, surface water ponds, storm and waste water collection systems, and systems permitted under other environmental laws. The regulations prescribe new tank standards, existing tank upgrading requirements which were scheduled for implementation over a period of years, tank operating requirements, release detection standards, release investigation requirements, corrective actions, closure requirements and financial responsibility requirements. The UST program is one of the broadest environmental programs and has been supplemented by numerous state and local laws that are different and sometimes stricter than the federal program. As a result, UST requirements are of special concern to buyers of industrial property and mortgage lenders who may have to foreclose on properties containing regulated USTs. 40 C.F.R. Parts 280 and 281.

Because the definition of a UST includes any one or a combination of tanks at a facility which are 10% or more beneath the ground surface, many owners and operators who thought they were not subject to RCRA have found belatedly that they were in violation. Because the definition includes connected underground pipes, it can also be difficult to distinguish storage tanks from process equipment.

The USEPA proposed an exemption from compliance with the hazardous waste requirements for material contaminated by petroleum from underground storage tanks. 58 Fed. Reg. 8,504 (2/12/93). See 40 C.F.R. § 261.4(b)(10).

In December 1994, the USEPA issued a final rule adopting standards further reducing emissions of organics from tanks, surface impoundments and containers at TSD facilities. 59 Fed. Reg. 62,896 (12/6/94); See various provisions in 40 C.F.R. Parts 264 and 265 and especially § § 264.1080 *et seq.* and 265.1080 *et. seq.*

I.   "Land Ban" Regulations

Between 1986 and 1990, the USEPA adopted a major program mandated by 1984 RCRA amendments to phase out land disposal of untreated hazardous wastes in three phases. The first phase of the regulations banned in 1986 the land disposal of wastes containing dioxins and certain solvents. The second phase banned in 1987 a list of wastes previously banned by the State of California.

The "California List" wastes included cyanides, some heavy metals, acids below 2.0 pH, PCB fluids, and liquid hazardous wastes containing halogenated organic compounds at elevated levels. The third phase included all other hazardous wastes divided into three categories commonly called the first-third, second-third and third-third rules. Under the land ban regulations, the USEPA set treatment standards for wastes upon the best demonstrated available technology (BDAT). The third-third rules issued in May 1990 addressed treatment standards and land disposal restrictions for many wastes including those mixed with radioactive and hazardous materials and the four "characteristic" wastes mentioned above. 40 C.F.R. Part 268.

Controversy has surrounded the level of pretreatment required by the USEPA before hazardous waste is eligible for land disposal. The U.S. District Court for the District of Columbia ruled that the USEPA's regulations must not only require pretreatment to remove the hazard characteristic of a hazardous waste but also to minimize hazardous constituents present in sufficient concentrations to pose short and long-term threats to human health or the environment. *Chemical Waste Management v. EPA*, 976 F.2d 2 (D.C. Cir. 1993).

J.   Medical Waste

RCRA sponsors a medical waste tracking program in which the USEPA and several states participate. 42 U.S.C. §§ 6912 and 6992; 40 C.F.R. Part 259.

VII. THE COMPREHENSIVE ENVIRONMENTAL RESPONSE, COMPENSATION AND LIABILITY ACT

A.   General

The Comprehensive Environmental Response, Compensation and Liability Act (CERCLA), 42 U.S.C. § 9601 *et seq.*, authorizes the USEPA to clean up contaminated facilities where there is a release or threatened release of hazardous substances, pollutants or contaminants. CERCLA also creates a multi-billion dollar trust fund (the "Superfund") derived from excise taxes on oil and chemical feedstocks and other sources for the use of the USEPA in cleanup and other response actions.

CERCLA requires any person in charge of a vessel or facility to report my release of a reportable quantity of a hazardous substance from the vessel or facility to the National Response Center. 42 U.S.C. §§ 9602 and 9603. The USEPA has issued an extensive list of hazardous substances and reportable quantities at 40 C.F.R. § 302.

B. Definition of a Hazardous Substance

The term "hazardous substance" is very broadly defined in CERCLA and includes substances designated as such by the USEPA under the CAA, CWA, RCRA and the Toxic Substances Control Act (TSCA) including any waste designated as hazardous waste under RCRA. Petroleum and natural gas are excluded. 42 U.S.C. § 9601(14); 40 C.F.R. Part 302. The courts have held that materials containing low levels of hazardous substances are subject to CER-CLA even though they are below the quantity or concentration levels and reportable quantities established for hazardous waste under the RCRA standards. *U.S. v. Alcan Aluminum Corp.*, 990 F.2d 711 (2d Cir. 1993); *U.S. v. Alcan Aluminum Corp.*, 964 F.2d 252 (3d Cir. 1992). Only a few courts have found any substance to be nonhazardous. The practical effect of these questionable decisions is that thousands of persons who sent ordinary solid waste to municipal and other landfills have been forced to pay large legal fees and liability settlements, although recently courts have granted relief to some defendants such as very small businesses. *B.F. Goodrich v. Murtha*, 815 F. Supp. 539 (D.C. Conn. 1993); later proceedings in the same case 840 F.Supp. 180 (D.C. Conn. 1994).

The courts have disagreed in interpreting the petroleum exclusion. For example, one court interpreted it broadly to cover gasoline. *Wilshire Westwood Associates v. Atlantic Richfield Co.*, 881 F.2d 801 (9th Cir. 1989). Other courts interpreted it narrowly and found distilled petroleum products and oil wastes to be hazardous substances. *U.S. v. Western Processing Co.*, 761 F. Supp. 713 (W.D.

Wash. 1991); *City of New York v. Exxon Corp.*, 744 F. Supp. 474 (S.D.N.Y. 1990).

CERCLA does not authorize response actions for a release or threatened release from products which are part of the structure of residential buildings or business or community structures. Accordingly, CERCLA does not authorize recovery of costs for removal of asbestos-containing materials from such buildings and structures. *First United Methodist Church v. U.S. Gypsum*, 882 F.2d 862 (4th Cir. 1989) and cases cited therein. The courts may reach the same result in lead-based paint cases.

C.   Releases

The USEPA can act when there is a release or a substantial threat of a release of a hazardous substance. A "release" means any spilling, leaking, pumping, pouring, emitting, emptying, discharging, injecting, escaping, leaching, dumping or disposing into the environment including abandonment of barrels, containers and other receptacles. Releases do not include releases solely within a workplace, vehicle engine exhausts, certain radioactive materials, normal fertilizer applications and federally permitted releases.

D.   Removal Actions

The USEPA can take immediate removal actions at any site where they are needed to prevent or mitigate immediate and significant risk of human life, health or the environment. The USEPA can also take planned removal actions limited in cost and time. 42 U.S.C. §§ 9601(23) and 9604(e). However, cleanup actions of a long term nature may be taken only at sites listed on the National Priority List.

E.   The National Contingency Plan

The USEPA has adopted a National Oil and Hazardous Materials Contingency Plan (NCP) which contains a Hazard Ranking System (HRS) for the selection of contaminated sites for cleanup and other response actions. Criteria in the HRS include the nature of the hazardous substances, conditions at the site, and the peril to health and the environment at the site and in neighboring communities.

Other factors to be considered include air, groundwater and surface water contamination pathways and toxicity including acute, chronic and carcinogenic effects. 55 Fed. Reg. 51,532 (12/14/90).

F.   The National Priority List

Sites receiving the highest ranking according to the HRS criteria are placed on the National Priority List (NPL). The NPL includes over 1,200 existing and proposed sites, including some sites in every state and many facilities owned or operated by the federal government. Many new sites are proposed each year. A cutoff score of 28.5 is used by the USEPA as a numerical criteria in deciding whether to list sites on the NPL. 40 C.F.R. Part 300, *et seq.*

It is possible to challenge a decision by the USEPA to list a site on the NPL by appealing to the U.S. Circuit Court of Appeals for the District of Columbia. For the first decade of CERCLA, no successful court challenges of NPL listings were made. However, there have been a few recent successes. *Tex Tin Corp. v. USEPA*, 935 F.2d 1321 (1991) and 992 F.2d 353 (1993); *Kent County v. USEPA*, 963 F.2d 391 (1992); *Anne Arundel County v. USEPA*, 963 F.2d 412 (1992); *National Gypsum Co. v. USEPA*, 968 F.2d 40 (1992).

G.   Remedial Actions

Remedial actions are permanent cleanup remedies. 42 U.S.C. § 9601(24). Among the more common remedial alternatives considered are soil removal; soil caps; slurry walls; soil treatment by such methods as biooxidation or vapor extraction; and groundwater treatment by pump and treat methods and other methods. Studies of innovative methods are also allowed. The alternatives at many NPL sites have been studied in extensive and repetitive detail over many years. Remediation of the NPL sites has been an important source of employment for environmental consultants and the legal profession.

H.   Steps to Accomplish Remediation

The remedial process begins with site identification which may result from fulfillment of reporting obligations, complaints or other sources. Once identified, sites are listed in the Comprehensive Environmental Response and Liability Information System (CERCLIS). The USEPA's steps to evaluate the site and subsequent steps appear in the computer accessible CERCLIS database. The USEPA conducts a preliminary assessment and may also conduct further investigations to determine whether the site will attain an HRS score high enough to support listing on the NPL.

The USEPA can itself perform both removal actions and remedial actions using moneys from the Superfund. The USEPA also has authority to issue administrative orders requiring private parties to abate, contain or remove releases of hazardous substances constituting an imminent and substantial danger. 42 U.S.C. § 9606. The USEPA does not usually perform response actions if a responsible party or parties are willing and qualified to do so. Accordingly, after initial investigation, the USEPA sends notices to potentially responsible parties (PRPs). It will also inform them of the kinds and volumes of wastes found at the site and the identity of the PRPs ranked by volume of waste. *See* Interim Settlement Policy, 50 Fed. Reg. 5,034 (2/5/85). *See also* OSWER Directive No. 7834.10, 53 Fed. Reg. 5,298 (2/23/88) on notice letters, negotiations and information exchange.

As described later, CERCLA imposes strict retroactive and usually joint and several liability on responsible parties to reimburse response costs of the USEPA. Private industrial companies designated as PRPs usually decide that they can perform response actions more effectively and at lower cost than the USEPA. Thus, the PRPs reserve their rights, but organize a PRP committee to represent them in negotiating to perform the response actions. They usually also organize one or more committees to represent them in negotiating liability settlements with the USEPA.

The PRP committee will negotiate an agreement with the USEPA for some or all the PRPs to perform and pay for remediation of the site. The agreement may also require the PRPs to perform or reimburse the cost of initial removal actions. Since 1986, the agreement is included in a consent decree entered in an enforcement action filed by the USEPA in a U.S. District Court. 42 U.S.C. § 9622. The USEPA published a model consent decree at 56 Fed. Reg. 30,996 (7/8/91) and said it would seldom negotiate changes.

The first major step in a remedial action is the preparation of a Remedial Action/Feasibility Study (RI/FS). Before authorizing a PRP Committee to perform an RI/FS, the USEPA must determine that it is qualified. The PRP committee must demonstrate that the PRPs can and will fund a substantial portion of cleanup cost. The PRP committee will hire an experienced environmental engineering firm to perform the RI/FS. At large or complex facilities, a work plan may precede the RI/FS.

The RI must be a full investigation including any remaining surface cleanup and tests of soil and groundwater by specified methods if storage or disposal was done at the site or if dumping, spills or leaks occurred. In the FS, alternate remediation proposals, ranging from minimal to optimal, must be discussed including implementation methods, feasibility, cost and effects on health and the environment. The RI/FS is presented to the USEPA which is required to select the least expensive alternative which is technologically feasible and reliable and which effectively mitigates and minimizes damage to, and provides adequate protection of, health, welfare and the environment. Treatment methods are favored over methods which remove waste or leave it in place. Any PRPs who disagree with the USEPA's selection cannot seek court review of the selection until the USEPA sues to recover its costs. 42 U.S.C. § 9613(h). Thus, PRPs must assume major risk if they wish to oppose the USEPA.

The USEPA must prepare and publish a Record of Decision explaining, among other things, its decision among the remedial alternatives. A public hearing is held at which state organizations are urged to participate and grants up to $50,000 are paid to public participants. When the remedial method is selected, a work plan is prepared for approval by the USEPA and is performed. It is difficult to challenge remedial decisions by the USEPA before it seeks to recover its response costs. However,, if it can be shown that the USEPA's remedy is arbitrary and would worsen the contamination, an injunction may be obtained. *U.S. Princeton Gamma Tech. Inc.*, No. 93-5252, 1994 U.S. App. Lexis 19, 885 (3d Cir. 8/1/94

When the remediation is fully performed, the PRPs who contributed to the cleanup are given limited releases ("covenants not to sue") by the USEPA, usually subject to reopening upon subsequent discovery of unknown conditions or new information indicating that the cleanup was not adequate. 52 Fed. Reg. 28,038 (7/27/87). However, a final release may be given in settlements with *de minimis* contributors and, in limited circumstances, to prospective purchasers of contaminated property. 42 U.S.C. § 9622(g); 52 Fed. Reg. 24,333 (6/30/87); 52 Fed. Reg. 43,393 (11/12/87); and 54 Fed. Reg. 34,235 (8/18/89).

I.   Remedy Selection Standards
      ("How Clean is Clean")

The statutory standards for selection of appropriate remedial actions are contained in CERCLA § 121. 42 U.S.C. § 9621. The remedy must protect human health and the environment, be cost-effective, and use permanent solutions and alternative treatment technologies or resource recovery technologies to the maximum extent practicable. The remedy must, to the extent practicable, be in accordance with the NCP. Important risk factors which must be considered include the persistence, toxicity, mobility, and the propensity to bioaccumulate of hazardous substances and their constituents. The USEPA may select an alternative remedial action even though it has not been achieved in practice at any other facility or site that has similar characteristics. In considering cost effectiveness, total long and short term costs, including operation and maintenance costs, must be considered. Offsite transport and disposal of hazardous substances or contaminants without treatment is disfavored. 42 U.S.C. § 9621.

As to the degree of cleanup, CERCLA § 121 provides that, if any hazardous substance, pollutant or contaminant will remain on-site, the remedial action selected must provide a level or standard of control which at least attains compliance with each applicable or relevant and appropriate federal or state standard, requirement, criteria or limitation, whichever is more stringent. Among other things, the remedy must provide a level or standard of control which at least attains the maximum contaminant level goals (MCLGs) under the Safe Drinking Water Act (SDWA) and the water quality criteria under the Clean Water Act (CWA) where such goals or criteria are relevant and appropriate under the circumstances. However, alternate concentration limits for hazardous constituents in groundwater may be established after careful study of hydrologic, geologic and other factors bearing on human exposure. 42 U.S.C. § 9621(d).

The USEPA has included in the NCP a list of factors to be used in determining the applicable or relevant and appropriate requirement (ARAR) standards to be used at an NPL site. 40 C.F.R. § 300.400(q). The USEPA has also included threshold criteria, primary balancing criteria and modifying criteria to be used in remedy selection. 40 C.F.R. § 300.400(f). The threshold criteria are protection of human health and the environment and compliance with ARAR standards. A remedy must meet the threshold criteria to be seriously considered for selection. Among the alternative remedies that meet the threshold criteria, selection is then based on the primary balancing criteria, including cost, and the modifying criteria.

The requirement that remedies comply with the strictest federal or state ARAR standards has made the cleanup of NPL sites extremely complex and costly because the mandate is to upgrade an abandoned dump without setting objectives for future use and cleanup levels that are reasonably related to such use. As a result, the requirement of cost-effectiveness is applied to alternatives that are exceedingly costly and may also be unattainable. Among the proposals for amendment of CERCLA are provisions which would substitute standards based on existing and future use of a site (i.e., residential, commercial or industrial) for the ARAR standards in order to allow economical rehabilitation of older urban industrial areas to provide employment.

J.   Recovery of Response Costs

CERCLA authorizes the USEPA to recover its response costs to remediate facilities contaminated with hazardous substances from responsible parties. CERCLA imposes retroactive strict liability for response costs on owners, operators, certain arrangers for disposal, and certain transporters. 42 U.S.C. § 9607.

Although CERCLA does not expressly so provide, the courts have generally found that the liability is also joint and several which makes even persons responsible for small volumes of hazardous substances present at a contaminated site fully liable for the entire cleanup cost and related liability. CERCLA excuses acts of God, acts of war, and acts or omissions by a third party if the person seeking excuse proves exercise of all due care and proves that he could not have foreseen the conduct of the third party. This last defense is sometimes called the "innocent landowner" defense, but the owner must show that prior to purchase he made a diligent investigation of a kind likely to reveal any contamination.

It has become customary for prospective purchasers and mortgage lenders to arrange for a so-called phase 1 assessment of the environmental condition of a property prior to a purchase or loan. The purpose is to support a claim of the "innocent landowner" defense and also to determine whether the value of the property may be impaired by contamination or violations of environmental laws or regulations. In 1994, the American Society for Testing Materials, Inc. (ASTM) issued Standard Practice E-1527-94 defining good commercial and customary practice in the U.S. for conducting an environmental assessment. (See also ASTM E1528-93). If a phase 1 assessment reveals possible contamination or violations, it may be followed by a phase 2 assessment in which soil, groundwater and other sampling and testing is performed to verify and quantify the conditions found in the phase 1 assessment. OBSERVATION: The scope of a phase 1 assessment is limited to conditions affecting commercial properties. Its scope is not sufficient to evaluate environmental compliance by an ongoing industrial business.

The USEPA has followed an "enforcement first" policy which devotes its primary efforts to enforcement litigation rather than to cleanups financed from the Superfund trust. The USEPA justifies its policy by concluding that the high cleanup costs which it requires will eventually total $50 billion and will exceed the resources of the Superfund trust. *See* "A Management Review of the Superfund Programs", June, 1988. *See also* the "Potentially Responsible Party Search Manual, 1987".

PRPs often believe they have been mistakenly designated. For example, the USEPA has often designated PRPs based on minimal evidence such as the presence at the site of containers bearing a manufacturer's markings or labels, although a local customer who bought the product from the manufacturer was more likely to have been the person who arranged the disposal. The USEPA has also frequently designated persons who disposed of harmless solid waste such as salt water or waste which contained infinitesimal quantities of hazardous substances.

The imposition of joint and several liability by the courts makes it extremely risky for PRPs to defend mistaken or unjust claims for response costs. The reason is that many NPL sites have large volumes of hazardous waste whose source cannot be identified by any means. This creates a so-called "orphan share" of liability to be absorbed by the responsible parties. The "orphan share" is increased whenever the USEPA settles with PRPs for less than their fair share of the response costs at a site. It is a common strategy for major PRPs to move quickly to settlement before the USEPA has fully investigated a site. These PRPs hope to settle before the full extent of their liability is revealed. If they succeed, the "orphan share" is increased. Some PRPs may also seek to dominate a PRP committee and to direct the RI/FS and remedial actions in ways which minimize their liability and increase the "orphan share" to be borne by other PRPs.

At many sites, the PRP committees have been able to negotiate a voluntary settlement to share costs among the PRPs. The usual allocation method is volumetric. However, if a court makes the allocation, toxicity and several other factors (sometimes called "Gore Factors") may be considered. *Control Data Corp. v. S.C.S.C. Corp.*, No. 94-1875 (8th Cir. May 10, 1995). *De minimis* and other small PRPs who will not undertake the burden of sponsoring the cleanup must often pay a premium over their volumetric share. PRPs responsible for wastes (such as PCBs) requiring special cleanup costs will probably be called upon to pay them separately. Such voluntary settlements can save considerable time and cost, but are difficult to negotiate when the "orphan share" is large. PRPs faced with an "orphan share" liability which seems very unfair or beyond their means may decide to take the risk of litigation.

As a partial answer to the "orphan share" problem the USEPA is authorized to make "mixed funding" settlements in which PRPs agree to fund a substantial portion of the response costs and the USEPA funds the rest. The larger the portion offered by the settling PRPs and the stronger the case the USEPA believes it has against nonsettling PRPs, the more likely it is that a "mixed funding" settlement can be achieved. 53 Fed. Reg. 8,279 (3/14/88).

Recognizing the severe hardship of joint and several liability, a few U.S. Courts of Appeals have recently ruled that a responsible party should be given an opportunity to demonstrate that its wastes contained hazardous substances only at "background levels" or that its liability was divisible and capable of apportionment. *U.S. v. Alcan Aluminum Corp.*, 990 F.2d 711 (2d Cir. 1993); *U.S. v. Alcan Aluminum Corp.*, 964 F.2d 252 (3d Cir. 1992). In one recent case, a Court of Appeals ruled that a responsible party had met its burden of proof. *In the Matter of Bell Petroleum Services, Inc.*, 3 F.3d 889 (5th Cir. 1993).

The USEPA has become aware of some of the hardships and political repercussions created by its interpretation of CERCLA as expanded by the federal courts. On July 30, 1993, the USEPA issued OSWER Directive No. 9834.17 titled "EPA Guidance on CERCLA Settlements with De Micromis Waste Contributors" in which it described lawsuits by major PRPs against hundreds of alleged generators of very small amounts of waste seeking to recover response costs and contributions to response costs. Regional offices of the USEPA have discretionary authority to make settlements with *de micromis* parties that would bar such lawsuits.

K.   Contribution Rights

CERCLA contains provisions authorizing persons who incur response costs to recover contributions from other responsible parties. 42 U.S.C. § 9613(f). To help PRPs to resolve cost sharing problems, CERCLA authorizes the USEPA to prepare a nonbinding allocation of responsibility (NBAR), but it has been reluctant to do so. 52 Fed. Reg. 19,919 (5/28/87). The USEPA may also make separate settlements with PRPs who contributed minimal amounts of waste at the facility. 52 Fed. Reg. 24,333 (6/30/87). CERCLA provides that a party which has resolved its liability to the U.S. or a state in an administrative or judicially approved settlement shall not be liable for contribution claims regarding matters addressed in the settlement. 42 U.S.C. § 9613(f)(2). For information about the 3 year statute of limitations applicable to contribution claims, see *United Technologies Corporation et al. v. Browning-Ferris Industries, Inc. et al.*, 33 F.3d 96 (1st Cir. 1994); cert. den. No. 94-1079, Feb. 17, 1995, in which the author served as counsel for one of the successful defendants.

L.   The CERCLA Lien

CERCLA provides that the costs and damages for which a person is liable under § 107(a) to the U.S. shall constitute a lien in favor of the U.S. upon all real property which belongs to such person and is subject to or affected by a removal or remedial action. The lien arises at the later of (1) the time when the costs are first incurred by the United States or (2) the time when the person is provided written notice by certified or registered mail. As to third parties, the lien is subject to rights perfected before notice of the lien is filed in the appropriate office, as designated by state law, where the property subject to the lien is located. 42 U.S.C. § 9607(l). A federal court of appeals has held that the procedures for imposition of the lien violate constitutional due process requirements by failing to provide notice and a predeprivation hearing to a property owner. *Reardon v. U.S.*, 947 F.2d 1509 (1st Cir. 1991).

M.   Lender Liability

The courts have ruled that banks and other lenders may be held liable as an owner or operator if they foreclose a mortgage or exercise supervisory powers contained in a loan agreement in a manner which involves them in ownership or operation of a facility. Leading court decisions on these subjects are *U.S. v. Mirabile*, 15 E.L.R. 20,992 (E.D. Pa. 1985); *U.S. v. Maryland Bank & Trust Co.*, 632 F. Supp. 573 (D. Md. 1986); *U.S. v. Fleet Factors*, 901 F.2d 1550 (11th Cir. 1990); and *Giudice v. BFG Electroplating*, 732 F. Supp. 556 (W.D. Pa. 1989). A decision in favor of a security holder, a municipal port authority which served as issuer of industrial revenue bonds with only nominal responsibilities, was rendered in *In re Bergsoe Metal Corp.*, 910 F.2d 668 (9th Cir. 1990).

In 1993, the USEPA adopted a rule interpreting the security interest exemption afforded to lenders by Section 101(20) of CER-CLA. The rule clarified the exemption by describing lenders' latitude to protect a security interest, including freedom to engage in workout activities, provided that the borrower continued to be the ultimate decision maker for the facility. The rule clarified that the security interest exemption does not require a lender to meet the requirements of the "innocent landowner" defense by steps such as performing an environmental inspection or audit of the collateral when the loan is made. If foreclosure becomes necessary, the rule relieved a lender from liability if it did not participate in management prior to foreclosure and if it forecloses and sells or otherwise divests the property within 12 months. If the property is not divested within 12 months, the lender would not necessarily become liable, but should be prepared to demonstrate that it did not participate in management prior to foreclosure and is using reasonable efforts to divest and is not holding the property for investment. In divesting collateral, a lender must not outbid, reject or fail to act within 90 days of receipt upon a written bona fide offer of fair consideration. 40 C.F.R. §§ 330.1100 and 330.1105. The rule applied not only to CERCLA and not to RCRA or other federal and state laws. Unfortunately, the rule was held invalid by the U.S. Court of Appeals for the District of Columbia because the USEPA lacked authority to restrict private rights of action under CERCLA. *Kelley v. E.P.A.*, 15

F.3d 1100 (D.C. Cir. 1994); rehearing denied 25 F.3d 1088 (D.C. Cir. 1994); cert. den. (No. 94-752, January 17, 1995). However, the USEPA can use the concepts in the rule as a guide in its enforcement of CERCLA.

In 1994, The USEPA proposed a lender liability rule applicable to underground storage tanks, acting under broader statutory authority in RCRA. 59 C.F.R. 30448, 6/13/94.

An example of a state law adopting the same principles as the CERCLA lender liability rule is 13 NJSA § 58: 10-23g-4, enacted in New Jersey in May 1993.

N.   Parent Corporation and Shareholder Liability

Parent corporations are not ordinarily responsible under CERCLA for environmental liabilities of their subsidiaries. Shareholders also are not ordinarily responsible for corporate CERCLA liabilities. However, liability has been imposed on traditional *alter ego* or "veil piercing" theories and also in situations where a parent or shareholder is found to be an "operator", because of participation, in daily activities or pervasive control of operations. *Joslyn Manufacturing Corp. v. T.L. James & Co.*, 893 F.2d 80 (5th Cir. 1990); *U.S. v. Kayser-Roth Corp.*, 724 F. Supp. 15 (D. R.I. 1989); *Idaho v. Bunker Hill Co.*, 635 F. Supp. 665 (D. Idaho 1986). Some courts might apply a stricter standard. *U.S. v. Mottolo*, 695 F. Supp. 615 (D. N.H. 1988); *State of New York v. Shore Realty*, 759 F.2d 1032 (2d Cir. 1985).

O.   Officer, Director, and Employee Liability

Officers, directors, and enployees of a corporation are not ordinarily subject to CERCLA liabilities of a corporation. However, they can become liable by engaging in the activities of an operator. This means either active participation in day-to-day activities or pervasive overall control of such activities. *U.S. v. Shore Realty Corp.*, supra; *U.S. v. Northeastern Pharmaceutical & Chem. Co.*, 810 F.2d 726 (8th Cir. 1986), cert. den. 484 U.S. 848 (1987); *U.S. v. Dean*, 969 F.2d 187 (6th Cir. 1992); and *U.S. v. Surely Refining Co.*, No. 93-2699 (8th Cir. 12/28/94. *See U.S. v. Carolina Transformer Co.*,

978 F.2d 832 (4th Cir. 1992) which may be read as holding that authority to control is a sufficient basis for liability.

P.   Successor Liability

Corporations engaging in merger and acquisition transactions may become responsible under CERCLA for environmental liabilities of the acquired business.   If a corporation acquires another corporation by merger, the borrower succeeds by operation of law to all liabilities of the merged corporation including CERCLA liabilities. *NJDEP v. Ventron Corp.*, 94 N.J. 473, 468 A.2d 150 (1983); *Smith Land and Improvement Corporation v. Celotex Corporation*, 851 F.2d 86 (3d Cir. 1988); *U.S. v. Crown Roll Leaf Inc.*, 29 ERC 2018 (D. N.J. 1987; *Anspec Co. v. Johnson Controls, Inc.*, 922 F.2d 1240 (6th Cir. 1991).

If a corporation acquires a business from another corporation and assumes its liabilities, the borrower may be responsible for environmental liabilities of the acquired business even as to a plant sold some years previously. *Philadelphia Electric Co. v. Hercules*, 762 F.2d 303 (3d Cir. 1985), cert den. 474 U.S. 980 (1985).

If a corporation acquires assets and declines to assume liabilities in a good faith arm's length transaction, it should not ordinarily become responsible for the seller's CERCLA liabilities.   *U.S. v. Mexico Feed & Grains*, 980 F.2d 478 (8th Cir. 1992). However, some courts have imposed successor liability under CERCLA using an expanded de facto merger doctrine. *In re Acushnet River and New Bedford Harbor Proceedings*, 712 F. Supp. 1010 (D. Mass. 1989); *Philadelphia Electric Co.*, supra; *Louisiana-Pacific Corp. v. Asarco, Inc.*, 909 F.2d 1260 (9th Cir. 1990). A substantial continuity test has also been used to impose successor liability. *U.S. v. Carolina Transformer Co.*, 978 F.2d 832 (4th Cir. 1992).

Q.   Arranger and Transporter Liability

Any person who arranges for disposal or treatment of hazardous substances which it owns or possess by another party or entity at a facility, incineration vessel or site owned or operated by such party or entity is subject to liability for response costs and other costs and damages under CERCLA. 42 U.S.C. § 9607(a)(3). This includes any person who arranged with a transporter for transport to a disposal or treatment facility. This subsection has been widely used to impose strict liability without fault on waste generators who thought they had made lawful arrangements with licensed transporters, but discovered later that the transporter or the disposal site mishandled the waste. Unforseen and even criminal conduct by the transporter or disposal facility does not excuse the liability. However, defendants were recently held not liable as arrangers for disposal where they simply returned drums to a supplier and received return of their deposit on grounds that they had no intent to dispose of the residues in the drums. *U.S. v. Cello-Foil Products*, No. 1-92-CV-713, 1994 U.S. Dist. LEXIS 4185 (W.D. Mich. 3/17/94).

Any person who accepts or accepted any hazardous substance for transport to disposal or treatment facilities, incineration vessels or sites selected by such person from which there is a release is subject to liability for response costs and other costs and damages. 42 U.S.C. § 9607(a)(4). For example, a transporter who substantially participates in selection of the disposal site by actions such as furnishing a list of sites can be held liable for response costs. 42 U.S.C. § 9607; *Tippins v. USX Corp.*, No. 93-3609, 1994 U.S. App. LEXIS 24550 (3d Cir., Sept. 12, 1994.)

R.   Indemnification

Liability for response costs under CERCLA cannot be assigned or otherwise transferred. 42 U.S. § 9607(e). However, the courts have held that indemnification agreements against liability are not contrary to this restriction and may be valid and enforceable if they meet appropriate requirements for such agreements. See, e.g., *Harley-Davidson, Inc. v. Minstar, Inc.*, 41 F.3d 341 (7th Cir. 1994) and cases cited therein.

S.   Pending Legislation

Since enactment of CERCLA, few sites listed on the NPL have been fully remediated. Surveys have shown that more money has been spent on legal and consulting fees than on remediation.

Critics and supporters of CERCLA agree that it should be simplified and that resources should be devoted to realistic cleanup of hazardous waste sites.

Two bills, each titled the Superfund Reform Act of 1994 and containing similar (but not identical) provisions, were approved by committees of the Senate and House of Representatives and came close to enactment in 1994. All or parts of the bills may again be considered in 1995.

A centerpiece of the bills is the proposed establishment of an Environmental Insurance Resolution Fund (EIRF) to be funded by a new tax on premiums of liability insurers and reinsurers designed to raise $810,000 per year for 10 years. Litigation against liability insurers by persons seeking to recover cleanup and removal costs would be automatically stayed. Persons notified that they may be required to perform or pay for a cleanup or removal action would submit their claims with evidence of a valid insurance contract to the EIRF. The EIRF would make resolution offers to the claimants based on several factors including the history of court decisions on insurance coverage in the state whose law governs their policy coverage. The claimants could accept or decline the offers. If accepted, the EIRF would pay costs already incurred over a 10 year period and future costs on a current basis. If declined, the claimant could continue to litigate and the EIRF would reimburse the insurer up to the amount of the resolution offer and, if the offer exceeds the amount recovered, also the insurer's litigation costs.

The bills would provide for more state participation in the selection of facilities for the NPL and would also provide for state registries listing facilities believed or known to present a current or potential hazard to human health or the environment. The bills would also provide for the establishment of qualified voluntary response programs administered by state environmental agencies. Facilities remediated under these programs would not be listed on the NPL and the remediation would be presumed to have been conducted in compliance with the NCP.

The bills would also make changes in remedy selection methods and cleanup standards. The EPA would be required to issue national goals to be applied to all NPL facilities, expressed as a single numerical level for carcinogens and noncarcinogens. These goals would provide the basis for the adoption of protective concentration levels unless the achievement of the goals is technically infeasible or unreasonably costly. The EPA would be required to issue a national risk protocol for conducting risk assessments used to determine need for remedial action, to establish protective concentration limits, and to evaluate remedial alternatives for NPL facilities. The bills would require the EPA to establish, to the extent appropriate and practicable, standardized exposure scenarios, formulae and methodologies. The guidelines for risk assessment would be designed to result in final protection at the 90th exposure percentile of the affected population. Remedial actions for contaminated water that may be used for drinking water would be required to attain the MCLs and non-zero MCLGs established under the Safe Drinking Water Act, but alternate concentration levels would be allowed under specified circumstances.

In remedy selection, the bills would place treatment methods and containment and engineering controls on an equal level. However, treatment would continue to be preferred for "hot spots," meaning discrete areas within a facility containing contaminants which are in high concentrations, are highly mobile, cannot be reliably contained, or present a significant risk should exposure occur. In remedy selection, the EPA would be required to consider the reasonably anticipated future uses of land at a facility.

Liability and its allocation would be modified in several ways. A new exemption from owner liability would be provided for persons who acquire a facility by inheritance or bequest if they meet strict requirements. The "innocent purchaser" exemption would be continued, but subject to exceptions which would continue to make it difficult to obtain. New exemptions from arranger and transporter liability would be provided for (1) persons responsible for very small ("de micromis") quantities of hazardous waste at a facility, (2) owners, operators and lessees of residential property, and (3) some small businesses and small charitable organizations. With some exceptions, liability of fiduciaries would be limited to the assets of their trust or estate. Arranger and transporter liability of municipal solid waste generators would be limited to 10% of the overall liability for a facility. The EPA's secured lender liability rule would be reinstated as of the date of its original adoption by the EPA.

Liability would be imposed only on PRPs designated by the EPA. Liability would be allocated by a person elected by the PRPs from a list of persons approved by the EPA. The allocator would make a non-binding apportionment based on several factors including the amount, degree of toxicity and mobility of the waste contributed by each PRP and the degree of care and cooperation of each PRP. An opportunity for an expedited settlement would be given to "de minimis" parties whose volumetric contribution of materials containing hazardous substances was minimal, provided that such substances do not present toxic or hazardous effects significantly greater than other hazardous substances at the facility. The so-called "orphan share" of liability resulting from exemptions, inability to identify persons responsible for all hazardous waste at a facility, and inability of PRPs to pay would be allocated among the solvent PRPs proportionately. Up to $300 million of "orphan share" liabilities would be payable annually from the EIRF.

The EPA and Department of Justice would have limited authority to reject an allocation and require a second allocation. Each PRP would have 90 days to make a settlement offer based on its final allocation percentage plus a premium which the EPA could impose to cover its risk of litigation with non-settling PRPs. PRPs who settle would have no further liability to the EPA or other PRPs. Non-settling PRPs would have joint and several liability for all response costs not recovered through the settlements including the "orphan share." At any time prior to issuance of an allocation report, any group of PRPs could submit a private allocation which must be adopted if it (1) is a binding allocation of all past, present and future costs, (2) does not allocate any share to a nonsignatory or, as to any orphan share, unless the U.S is a signatory, and (3) the signatories waive contribution rights against other PRPs.

The bills were not adopted in 1994, but had extensive support and have been reproposed in 1995. Since the elections in late 1994 resulted in election of a Republican majority in both the Senate and

House of Representatives for the first time in 40 years, many changes are being considered with some bipartisan support, including possible repeal or limitation of strict retroactive liability and joint and several liability. In reauthorizing CERCLA, Congress may use a number of provisions from the 1994 bills to achieve compromises.

VIII. EMERGENCY PLANNING AND COMMUNITY RIGHT-TO-KNOW ACT

The Emergency Planning and Community Right-to-Know Act (EPCRA), 42 U.S.C. § 11001 *et seq.*, was adopted in 1986 as an amendment creating Title III of CERCLA. Impetus for enactment was partially provided by serious accidents in foreign countries, i.e., the methyl isocyanate leak at Bhopal, India and the nuclear reactor fire at Chernobyl, Russia.

Subtitle A (§§ 301-305) of EPCRA requires that states establish state emergency response commissions (SERCs), planning districts and local emergency planning committees (LEPCs) which must develop comprehensive emergency response plans including identification of facilities having extremely hazardous substances. 42 U.S.C. §§ 11001-11005. The plans must also establish methods and procedures to be followed by facility owners and operators and local emergency and medical personnel in responding to a release of extremely hazardous substances. The plans must include procedures for notifying safety officials and the public, personnel training programs and evacuation plans. The states have taken different regulatory attitudes. For example, New Jersey has 537 LEPCs while Georgia has a single statewide LEPC.

EPCRA required the USEPA to publish a list of extremely hazardous substances. The list appears (alphabetically and by CAS numbers) as Appendix A to 40 C.F.R. Part 355 and includes several hundred substances with the reportable quantity and the threshold planning quantity for each of them. A facility having any of these substances in excess of specified threshold levels must comply not only with the general CERCLA notification requirements but also must notify the SERC and LEPC of any release of an extremely hazardous substance beyond the boundaries of the facility. The

53

notice requirement, however, does not apply to releases within the limits of federal air and water permits and certain other continuous releases. The notice must include extensive information about the release, anticipated health risks, medical advice and precautions to be taken including evacuation. See 40 C.F.R. Part 355.

Subtitle B of EPCRA (42 U.S.C. §§ 11021-11023) establishes still broader programs. Section 11021 requires facilities having hazardous chemicals in excess of stated quantities to provide to the SERC, LEPC and local fire departments copies of the material safety data sheets (MSDS) required by the Occupational Safety and Health Act or a list of such chemicals containing MSDS information. These hazardous chemicals go beyond the list of extremely hazardous chemicals and include any chemical which is a physical hazard or health hazard. Chemicals which are physical hazards include flammables, combustibles, explosives, compressed gases, oxidizers, pyrophors and unstable or water reactive substances. Chemicals which are health hazards include those with acute effects (such as ammonia or chlorine) but also those with chronic effects including carcinogens, teratogens, mutagens, toxins and agents affecting blood, lungs and other organs. There are numerous exemptions, however, for consumer products, foods, drugs, cosmetics, household items, substances used in medical and research facilities and other substances including tobacco products. *See* 40 C.F.R. Part 370.

42 U.S.C. § 11022 requires facility owners or operators to prepare and submit to the SERC, LEPC, and fire department annually an inventory of hazardous chemicals, including quantity and location data, and other information. The USEPA's regulations on emergency and hazardous chemical inventory reporting, including the Tier I and Tier II reporting forms are at 40 C.F.R. Part 370.

Section 11023 requires facilities with 10 or more full-time employees and in Standard Industrial Codes 20 through 39 to report annually to the USEPA and state environmental agencies on releases of toxic chemicals that can reasonably be expected to cause adverse human health effects or significant adverse effects on the environment. Subject to quantity exemptions which decline each year, these reports must include permitted emissions of toxic chemicals because the reports will be used by the USEPA to maintain a national toxic chemical inventory and related database available to the public. The USEPA's regulations require the filing of a Toxic Chemical Release Inventory Reporting Form (Form R) which includes detailed information about chemical inventories and their use, disposal and any releases. See 40 C.F.R. Part 372 including the list of toxic chemicals at § 372.65. In 1994, the USEPA added 286 chemicals and two chemical categories to the list of toxic chemicals subject to the reporting requirements. 59 Fed. Reg. 61432 (11/30/94).

Subtitle C of EPCRA (42 U.S.C. §§ 11041-11050) contains general provisions including strictly limited rights to withhold trade secret information; provision of information to doctors, nurses and other health professionals; civil and criminal penalties and other enforcement provisions; and rights of citizens and state and local government agencies to sue for enforcement and damages.

IX. THE TOXIC SUBSTANCES CONTROL ACT

The Toxic Substances Control Act (TSCA), 15 U.S.C. § 2601 *et seq.*, regulates the manufacture, processing, distribution and disposal of chemical substances and mixtures. TSCA is administered primarily by the USEPA. TSCA applies to imports as well as substances and mixtures manufactured in the U.S. Except for notice provisions, TSCA does not apply to substances, mixtures and articles manufactured or processed solely for export and not for use in the United States.

A chemical substance is any organic or inorganic substance of a particular molecular structure including (i) any combination of such substances occurring in whole or in part as a result of a chemical reaction or occurring in nature and (ii) any element or uncombined radical. In general, a mixture is any combination of two or more substances if the combination does not occur in nature and is not, in whole or part, the result of a chemical reaction. Microorganisms and their DNA molecules are considered to be "chemical substances" by the USEPA. 51 Fed. Reg. 23,302 (6/26/86), 49 Fed. Reg. 50,886 (12/31/84).

TSCA does not apply to pesticides, tobacco products, certain nuclear materials, firearms, foods, drugs and cosmetics because all of these substances (except tobacco products) are subject to other regulatory laws. The tobacco industry is a major industry in the southeastern U.S. which also has considerable freedom from product liability laws applied to other industries.

Section 4 of TSCA authorizes the USEPA, by rule, to require testing of chemical substances or mixtures, subject to detailed criteria. In the case of mixtures, testing is required only if the USEPA finds the effects may not reasonably and more efficiently be determined by testing the chemical substances which comprise the mixture. A priority list of chemical substances is listed at 40 C.F.R. § 712.30. Good laboratory practice standards are prescribed at 40 C.F.R. Part 792. Test guidelines are contained in 40 C.F.R. Parts 795 through 799.

Testing under Section 4 is often arranged under a consent agreement between the USEPA and members of an industry who agree to conduct satisfactory tests. These industry members will agree among themselves on cost sharing. Other industry members can seek an exemption on grounds that satisfactory testing is in progress. However, the exempted companies must reimburse the companies who perform the testing. If they do not reach a voluntary agreement, the USEPA will order them to pay fair and equitable compensation. To resolve disputes, any party can request resolution by the American Arbitration Association (AAA). The USEPA will then base its order on the AAA's decision. Processors may be excluded from the obligation to reimburse because they will usually absorb the cost as manufacturers increase prices to reflect the test costs and any resulting product improvements.

The cost sharing provisions of Section 4 of TSCA resulted from industry protests that the burden of testing ordered by the USEPA should be shared by all members of an industry that manufactures, imports or processes a chemical substance. The same reasoning applies to companies who benefit from testing performed by the first company to submit a pre-manufacturing notice.

Section 5 of TSCA requires a 90-day pre-manufacturing notice (PMN) to the USEPA before (1) manufacturing or processing of a new chemical substance or (2) manufacturing or processing any chemical substance for a use determined by the USEPA to be a significant new use. A new chemical substance is any not included in an inventory list of over 58,000 chemical substances compiled by the USEPA during 1979 and 1980. The list is periodically updated by corrections, additions of new chemical substances which have cleared the PMN process, and subtractions of chemical substances no longer manufactured or imported. Over 70,000 chemical substances are now listed in the inventory. See 40 C.F.R. Parts 710 and 720.

Mixtures are not subject to the PMN requirement. USEPA regulations provide exceptions for small research and development quantities, certain impurities and byproducts, chemicals produced from inadvertent reactions and nonisolated intermediaries. A special "polymer" exemption and a test marketing exemption are also available, but require an application and review by the USEPA prior to commencement. See 40 C.F.R. Parts 720 and 723.Section 5 also authorizes the USEPA to require by rule that chemical substances applied to significant new uses comply with the PMN requirements. The EPA's signficant new use rules are called SNURs. 40 C.F.R. Part 721.

In 1994, the USEPA amended Parts 704, 720, 721 and 723 to simplify and reduce the costs and burdens of PMN compliance. Among other actions, the USEPA expanded the "polymer" exemption and the exemption for chemical substances manufactured in small quantities (10,000 kg per year) or having low environmental releases or human exposures. 60 Fed. Reg. 16,346, 3/29/95.

Section 6 of TSCA authorizes the USEPA to impose restrictions if it finds there is reasonable basis to conclude that the manufacture, processing, distribution, use or disposal of a chemical substance will result in an unreasonable risk of injury to health or the environment. These include prohibition of the substance or mixture, limitation on concentrations in manufacture or use, warning labels and instructions, record keeping, limitations on use, prohibition or regulation of disposal, and notice and recall or repurchase. The Act requires the USEPA to apply the *least* burdensome requirements to the extent necessary to protect adequately against the risk. If the risk is being caused inadvertently, the USEPA may review the quality control procedures of a manufacturer or processor.

Section 6 of TSCA authorizes the USEPA to commence action in a U.S. District Court for seizure of any imminently hazardous chemical substance or mixture and to seek relief against any person who manufactures, processes, distributes, uses or disposes of any such substance or mixture or article containing the same.

Section 8 of TSCA requires record keeping and reporting. Most important, records of "significant adverse reactions" alleged to have been caused by a chemical substance or mixture must be made. Allegations made by or on behalf of employees must be recorded and retained for 30 years and those by or on behalf of other persons for 5 years. A "significant adverse reaction" means a reaction that may indicate a substantial impairment of normal activities, or long-lasting or irreversible damage to health or the environment. USEPA rules clarifying these recordkeeping and reporting obligations are at 40 C.F.R. Part 717. New health and safety studies must also be reported. 40 C.F.R. Part 716.

Section 8(e) of TSCA requires that any person who manufactures, processes or distributes a chemical substance or mixture and who obtains information which reasonably supports that it represents a substantial risk of injury to health or the environment shall immediately inform the USEPA unless such person has actual knowledge that the USEPA has been actually informed of such information. A company is considered to have received information when received by an officer or employee capable of appreciating its significance. Most companies have established internal reporting systems headed by committees to screen information and determine whether it is reportable. Such a system relieves officers and employees of the obligation to report directly to the USEPA. A Statement of Interpretation and Enforcement Policy was issued in 1978 by USEPA providing guidelines on Section 8(e). 43 Fed. Reg. 11,110 (1978). During 1990 and 1991, the USEPA initiated strict enforcement steps against several manufacturers based on interpretations that industry claimed were new, but the USEPA claimed were consistent with its 1978 Policy. See EPA Guidance Document dated January 3, 1990, *BNA Environmental Law Reporter*, 1/12/90.

TSCA prohibits the manufacture and distribution of poly-chlorinated biphenyls (PCBs) in any manner other than a totally enclosed manner, except as authorized by USEPA rules prescribing warnings, instructions and disposal methods. PCB fluids were widely used as heat transfer media and as dielectric fluids in electrical transformers and capacitors. Because of their stability, they do not readily biodegrade and are listed as hazardous primarily because of their teratogenic effects on birds and small animals. Limited testing of highly chlorinated PCB fluids was used to list all PCBs as suspect carcinogens although tests of lower-chlorinated PCBs have not shown carcinogenicity. The USEPA has adopted PCB rules applicable to electrical equipment and to closed manufacturing and closed waste manufacturing processes. 40 C.F.R. Part 761. The USEPA has also adopted a rule defining "significant exposure" and "totally enclosed manner." The USEPA has also adopted a cleanup policy for PCB spills. 52 Fed. Reg. 10,688 (4/7/87).

X. LAWS RELATING TO ASBESTOS CONTAINING MA-TERIALS

The Asbestos Hazard Emergency Response Act (AHERA), 15 U.S.C. § 2641-2656, is an amendment to TSCA. It requires the USEPA to adopt regulations requiring the inspection of schools for asbestos containing materials and appropriate remedial action; accreditation of asbestos abatement contractors; periodic reinspection after abatement actions; and a study of the alleged danger to human health posed by asbestos in public and commercial buildings. The USEPA's asbestos regulations under TSCA are at 40 C.F.R. § 763.60 *et seq.*

Asbestos is a natural fibrous mineral mined in Canada, the United States, South Africa, Russia and a few other nations. It is an excellent fire retardant and heat resistant material used historically in a wide range of applications including insulation of boilers and pipes, steel construction materials, ceiling and floor tiles, roofing materials, and brake linings.

Asbestos is considered to be hazardous when it is "friable", thus creating a risk that fibers will become airborne and will be inhaled in excessive quantities. Fully encapsulated asbestos is not hazardous so long as it remains nonfriable.

There are several forms of asbestos. Among them are chrysotile (white), crocidolite (blue), amosite (brown) and anthophyllite. Each has different characteristics and the hazard levels differ for each. However, there has been no recognition of the hazard differences under AHERA or other laws and regulations.

Although safely used by many industrial asbestos manufacturers and users for many years, asbestos was widely misused in shipyards operated by and for the U.S. Government during World War II and the Korean War. The misuse caused asbestosis among many workers. Asbestos also caused mesothelioma, a rare disease, and was reported in studies by researchers at Mt. Sinai Medical Center to have contributed to lung cancers among workers, especially those who were smokers or whose lungs were subject to other respiratory stresses. The U.S. Government declined to accept responsibility and was eventually upheld by the federal courts. Thousands of lawsuits were filed against manufacturers of asbestos-containing materials on behalf of workers in many industries claiming bodily injuries and by property owners claiming abatement costs. The lawsuits were based on strict liability including failure to warn of asbestos hazards. The manufacturers commenced numerous lawsuits against their liability insurers. In recent years, the lawsuits included many workers suffering primarily from tobacco smoking. Billions of dollars have been recovered in these lawsuits and bankruptcies of several manufacturers and insurers have resulted. For example, asbestos liabilities contributed significantly to the need to reorganize the underwriting syndicates at Lloyds in the City of London.

Recognizing that unsupervised removal of asbestos could create hazards for workers and building occupants, AHERA requires accreditation programs for contractors and laboratories that include air testing by electron microscope, surveillance, reinspections, warning labels, education, use of respirators and other personal protective equipment and proper disposal of asbestos containing wastes.

AHERA allows encapsulation and other preventive measures designed to eliminate damage, deterioration or delamination but the cost of continued monitoring, reinspection and other steps often lead to a decision to abate by removal.

AHERA presently does not require remediation of nonschool public buildings and does not apply to privately owned buildings or homes. However, environmentalists, plaintiff attorneys, labor unions and asbestos removal contractors have urged extension of AHERA to include all public buildings. Thus far, Congress has declined to do so, because costs may well exceed benefits and because many buildings are being remediated voluntarily or in response to state law or NESHAP requirements.

Asbestos-related activities are also regulated by the USEPA under the CAA in a NESHAP found at 40 C.F.R. § 61.140 *et seq.* The USEPA enforces the NESHAP strongly against contractors who fail to comply with its "wetting" and other requirements during demolition and renovation operations.

In 1990, the USEPA published a useful book called "Managing Asbestos in Place - A Building Owner's Guide to Operations and Maintenance Programs for Asbestos Containing Materials." The book, called the "Green Book," acknowledges that the average airborne asbestos levels in buildings and, accordingly, the health risk to building occupants seems to be very low. Thus, it recommends management in place rather than removal except during building demolition, renovation or other activities which would cause asbestos to become airborne and create health risk.

Employers must protect employees from exposure to asbestos in the workplace by complying with comprehensive regulations of the Occupational Safety and Health Administration (OSHA). See the OSHA General Industry Standard at 29 C.F.R. § 1910.1001 and the Construction Standard at 29 C.F.R. § 1926.58. OSHA recently amended both Standards to impose certain responsibilities on building owners and operators as well as employees.

Asbestos is also regulated by the CWA (40 C.F.R. Part 427); other provisions of TSCA (40 C.F.R. § 763.60); and the solid waste provisions of RCRA (40 C.F.R. Part 258). Asbestos is listed as a hazardous substance under CERCLA (40 C.F.R. § 302.4). Transportation of asbestos is regulated by the Hazardous Materials Transportation Act. 49 U.S.C. § 1801 *et seq.*; 49 C.F.R. Parts 172, 173 and 177 and the Sanitary Food Transportation Act of 1990, 49 U.S.C. § 2801 *et seq.* Further, some state and local laws apply to public and private buildings such as Local Ordinance No. 76 of The City of New York and the regulations thereunder.

In 1989, the USEPA announced a rule prohibiting the manufacture, importation, processing and distribution of most asbestos-containing products to take effect in three stages over a period of years including roofing, flooring and brake-lining materials in which asbestos is fully encapsulated. However, most of the rule was vacated in *Corrosion Proof Fittings v. E.P.A.*, 947 F.2d 1201 (5th Cir. 1991). In 1993, the USEPA published its determinations of the parts of the rule remaining in effect and said that it expected to publish an amended rule in the near future to bring the rule in line with the court ruling.

XI. THE SAFE DRINKING WATER ACT

The Safe Drinking Water Act (SDWA), 42 U.S.C. § 300f *et seq.*, requires the USEPA to set standards for contaminants in drinking water. The drinking water standards apply to public water systems which provide piped water for human consumption having at least 15 service connections or regularly serving at least 25 individuals, but excluding hotels and other storage and distribution facilities which obtain water from a public water system. The states have primary enforcement responsibility for the SDWA, provided that they adopt regulations as strict as those of the USEPA and meet other requirements set by the USEPA.

The SDWA establishes some requirements directly. For example, the SDWA requires that pipe, solder or flux used after June

19, 1986 in construction or repair of any public water system be lead free. It also requires that treatment of synthetic organic chemicals must be at least as effective as that achievable by granular activated carbon adsorption technology.

The SDWA also applies to underground injection control (UIC) programs to protect drinking water from contamination by disposal of hazardous waste into underground deep well disposal facilities. The SDWA also includes wellhead protection programs and sole source aquifer protection programs to protect groundwater used as drinking water.

The USEPA has adopted primary and secondary drinking water standards. The primary standards are health-based standards which apply to contaminants found in drinking water that may have an adverse effect on human health. The secondary standards are not health-based and are issued as guidelines to state agencies in relation to substances which may adversely affect the odor or appearance of water or may cause a substantial number of persons to discontinue use. They are not enforceable by the USEPA against public water systems.

Through 1986, the USEPA set maximum contaminant limits (MCLs) for several partially soluble heavy metals, trihalomethanes, coliform bacteria, turbidity and radiation. It also set secondary standards for some additional contaminants and established sampling and analytical methods. The USEPA also published recommended maximum contaminant limits (RCMLs) for a number of contaminants.

In 1986, Congress adopted amendments to the SDWA requiring the USEPA to accelerate adoption of primary drinking water regulations and to establish standards for the filtration and disinfection of drinking water drawn by public water systems. The USEPA published the required rules at 54 Fed. Reg. 27,486 (6/29/89); 40 C.F.R. Part 141. The implementation cost was estimated at $3 billion.

After 1986, the USEPA adopted drinking water MCLs standards at a faster pace. Of special interest to industry, *see* 56 Fed. Reg.

3,526 (1/30/91), 56 Fed. Reg. 26,460 (6/7/91), 56 Fed. Reg. 30,266 (7/1/91), and 57 Fed. Reg. 31,776 (7/17/92). See also 40 C.F.R. Part 141. The USEPA also published and updated a drinking water priority list. 53 Fed. Reg. 1,892 (1/22/88) and 56 Fed. Reg. 1,470 (1/14/91).

The SDWA contains very strict procedures for determining standards. The procedures begin with setting maximum contaminant level goals (MCLGs) which are nonenforceable. They are based on reference doses derived from no observed adverse effect levels (NOAELs) which are derived from studies which are often quite limited and suggest adverse effects based on modest evidence. The MCLGs tend to be set at extremely low levels. For substances which environmental researchers suspect to be carcinogens, the MCLG is set at zero. The USEPA then sets the MCL as close to the MCLG as can be achieved by the best available technology, taking into account cost and effectiveness in actual operation. The SDWA allows public water systems to apply for variances and exemptions from compliance with the MCLs, but they are for short periods and are not easily obtained.

The USEPA's regulations include extensive and detailed monitoring and analytical requirements as well as recordkeeping, public notification and reporting requirements. 40 C.F.R. Part 141. The multibillion dollar burdens of these requirements on public water systems were among the reasons why state and local governments have complained to Congress about "unfunded mandates."

Legislation to reauthorize the SDWA was almost adopted in 1994, but failed in the last hours of the Congressional session. The legislation would have repealed the mandatory schedule to regulate 25 new contaminants annually and would have required use of sounder scientific methods in selecting contaminants for regulation. The legislation would also have provided major funding to enable community water systems to perform their obligations. The legislation has been reintroduced in 1995.

XII. FEDERAL INSECTICIDE, FUNGICIDE AND RODEN- TICIDE ACT

The Federal Insecticide, Fungicide and Rodenticide Act (FI-FRA), 7 U.S.C. § 136 *et seq.*, was originally enacted in 1947, and granted authority to the U.S. Department of Agriculture (USDA) which then administered it. The administration of FIFRA was transferred to the USEPA in 1970. As amended in 1972 and thereafter, FIFRA requires the registration of pesticides with the USEPA and prohibits sale, receipt and other transfers of unregistered pesticides. FIFRA also regulates traps and other devices (except firearms) used for pest, animal and plant control. USEPA regulations are at 40 C.F.R. Parts 152 *et seq.*

A pesticide is any substance or mixture intended for preventing, destroying, repelling or mitigating any pest or as a plant regulator, defoliant or desiccant. Thus, the definition includes herbicides, rodenticides and other economic poisons. Certain articles are excluded such as substances regulated by the Food and Drug Administration. Pesticides contribute importantly to the abundance of food that has made famines a rarity (except during wars) in the world which once feared starvation resulting from population growth.

Establishments producing pesticides and their ingredients must also be registered with the USEPA and are subject to inspection, recordkeeping and reporting requirements. FIFRA also authorizes the USEPA to review and approve state programs for the certification of pesticide applicators and to conduct certification programs for applicators in states not having an approved plan. Restricted pesticides may be applied only by persons who are certified applicators on property other than their own property.

All new pesticide products, with few exceptions, must be registered with the USEPA. Registration of a pesticide requires the applicant to file (1) its label including a statement of all claims made for the pesticide and directions for its use, (2) a description of tests and results on which claims for the pesticide are based, (3) the complete formula, and (4) a request for classification for general or restricted use, or both. Limited trade secret protection is available.

The USEPA must approve an application for registration of a pesticide if (1) its composition warrants the proposed claims, (2) its labelling and other submitted materials comply with FIFRA, (3) it will perform its intended function without unreasonable adverse effects on the environment, and (4) it will not generally cause unreasonable adverse effects when used in accordance with widespread and generally recognized practice. Each registration is for specific uses and is for a period of five years, after which it expires unless renewed. Renewal is not automatic and the USEPA may request additional safety information in considering a renewal.

FIFRA imposes detailed labelling requirements (including the familiar "skull and crossbones" and "poison" warnings) and a statement of practical treatment (first aid or otherwise) in case of poisoning. FIFRA prohibits claims and compositions which differ from the registration. FIFRA also prohibits a variety of other practices including miscoloring, misbranding, adulteration and misadvertising; use of a pesticide in a manner inconsistent with its labeling; and use of a pesticide classified for restricted use for other purposes. FIFRA applies to imports and also contains limited provisions applicable to exports. Unregistered pesticides can be exported subject to several conditions including notice to the applicable foreign government and appropriate international agencies.

A major FIFRA program has been the reregistration of many pesticides granted registration when standards were more lenient. Many older pesticides have been discontinued by their manufacturers or denied registration as a result of inability to meet new standards or to bear the cost of reregistration.

The USEPA is authorized to commence proceedings to cancel a registration if it believes that a pesticide presents a substantial question of safety to man or the environment. The USEPA can also suspend (i.e., impose an immediate prohibition on production and distribution) a pesticide if it finds it is an "imminent hazard" which the U.S. Circuit Court of Appeals for the District of Columbia has interpreted as merely a finding of a serious threat to public health including animals and fish. If a registration is suspended or canceled because of an imminent hazard, FIFRA authorized indemnity payments to end users, dealers and distributors under some circumstances. Millions of dollars were paid as indemnities for cancellation of the registrations of ethylene dibromide, 2,4,5-T/Silvex and dinoseb.

The USEPA may order manufacturers to recall a pesticide when its registration is cancelled or suspended, but often allows existing inventories to be used for some period of time. See 40 C.F.R. § 165.

In 1988, amendments to FIFRA were adopted to make its provisions much stricter, although less strict than environmental advocates urged. The reregistration process for all pesticides registered before November 1, 1984 was accelerated. During 1989, the USEPA published lists of active ingredients according to priorities based on the possibility that the pesticides would contaminate food or animal feed or leach into groundwater. Companies wishing to maintain registration were required to provide extensive data within a year including tests, studies and any adverse information about the active ingredient. In October 1990, the USEPA published a list of some 1,100 pesticide registration requests for cancellation and many more cancellations have followed in subsequent years. Many cancellations were of older products no longer used or unable to compete with newer products. However, the extraordinary registration fees and the burden of the registration requirements upon small businesses contributed to these cancellations. Fees were increased to between $50,000 and $100,000 for a new registration and $75,000 and $150,000 for a reregistration. Annual maintenance fees are $650 for the first product, subject to limits for companies having multiple registrations.

The 1988 amendments contained provisions intended to simplify and accelerate the registration of generic pesticide products. Other 1988 amendments rescinded indemnity payments to manufacturers and limited payments to dealers and distributors. They also authorized the USEPA to adopt storage, transport and packaging regulations including design, use, reuse and disposal of containers. They also eliminated any responsibility of the USEPA to share costs of recall and disposal of suspended and cancelled pesticides. Criminal penalties for violations were increased.

The USEPA has adopted extensive regulations implementing FIFRA. They include labelling and packaging standards, good laboratory practices standards, certification of usefulness, disposal and storage, worker protection, and tolerances (maximum residue limits) for pesticides used in or on raw agricultural commodities and in food and animal feeds. 40 C.F.R. Parts 152 to 186. FIFRA requires the packaging standards set by the USEPA be consistent with those established under the Poison Prevention Packaging Act which protects children from poisoning by inadequately packaged drugs or other toxic products used in households. 15 U.S.C. § 1471 *et seq.*

The use of some pesticides has been placed in doubt by the so-called "Delaney Amendment", a provision added in 1958 to 21 U.S.C. § 321 (s) of the Federal Food, Drug, and Cosmetic Act (FFDCA), 21 U.S.C. § 301 *et seq.* The provision states that no food additive shall be deemed safe if it is found to induce cancer when ingested by man or animal. For some time, the USEPA adopted tolerances which allowed the use of negligible amounts of pesticides found to cause cancer in laboratory animals. However, environmental organizations obtained a court order setting aside the USEPA's regulations on grounds that the Delaney Amendment sets a "zero tolerance" level which allows no discretion to the USEPA. *Les v. Reilly*, 968 F.2d 985 (9th Cir. 1992). Congress is currently considering legislation which would revoke the Delaney Amendment and establish a negligible risk standard for pesticide residues in both raw and processed food.

The USEPA has adopted agricultural worker protection standard under FIFRA, 40 C.F.R.. Parts 156 and 170, See proposed amendments at 60 Fed Reg. 21960, 5/3/95.

Although the court decisions are not entirely clear, it appears that FIFRA does not preempt state and local laws regulating pesticides except for those which require labelling or packaging in addition to or different from those required by FIFRA. *Wisconsin Public Intervenor v. Mortier*, 111 S.Ct. 2476 (1991); *Papas v. Zoecon Corporation*, 926 F.2d 1019 (11th Cir. 1991); vacated and remanded

112 S.Ct. 3020, 120 L.Ed.2d 892 (1992). Thus, a number of states and municipalities have adopted their own laws and regulatory programs which supplement FIFRA and the federal courts have upheld them. However, since 1992, the federal courts have continued to reach a variety of results in cases involving preemption issues where state law is alleged to involve labelling or packaging, especially in tort cases. Six federal appellate courts have found that tort law claims based on alleged inadequacy of the warning labels prescribed by FIFRA were preempted. *King v. E.I. Du Pont*, 996 F.2d 1346 (1st Cir. 1993); *Worm v. American Cyanamid*, 5 F.3d 744 (4th Cir. 1993); *McDonald v. Monsanto Co.*, 27 F.3d 1021 (5th Cir. 1994); *Shaw v. Dow Brands, Inc.*, 994 F.2d 364 (7th Cir. 1993); *Arkansas Platte & Gulf v. Van Waters & Rogers*, 981 F.2d 1177 (10th Cir. 1993); and *Papas v. Upjohn Co.*, 985 F.2d 516 (11th Cir. 1993). However, see an unusual decision to the contrary in *Ferebee v. Chevron Chemical Co.*, 736 F.2d 1529 (9th Cir. 1984); cert den. 469 U.S. 1062 (1984).

XIII. HAZARDOUS MATERIALS TRANSPORTATION ACT

The Hazardous Materials Transportation Act (HMTA), 49 U.S.C. § 5101 *et seq.* (formerly § 1801 *et seq.*), requires that shippers, transporters and persons who manufacture, sell or perform services related to packages or containers of hazardous, radioactive or explosive materials in excess of specified quantities must file a registration statement with the U.S. Department of Transportation (DOT) which has administered the HMTA for many years. Although little known to the general public, the programs and experience of the DOT and its Research and Special Programs Administration (RSPA) have long provided expert and important protection of public safety.

Hazardous materials are substances and materials in quantities or forms that pose an unreasonable risk to health and safety or property when transported in commerce. They include, without limitation, explosives, radioactive materials, etiological agents, flammable liquids or solids, poisons, oxidizing or corrosive materials, and compressed gases.

Hazardous materials include hazardous waste. 49 C.F.R. §§ 171.3 and 171.8. The definition of hazardous waste is any waste subject to the manifest requirements of RCRA specified in 40 C.F.R. Part 262.

Under the HMTA and earlier laws, the DOT has adopted regulations creating a comprehensive system for the safe transportation of hazardous materials by rail, aircraft, vessel and public highway. 49 C.F.R. Parts 171-*180*. The DOT regulations prescribe test methods to determine hazards such as "flash point" tests to determine flammability. They require warning labels on containers and packages and warning placards on vehicles. They prescribe specifications for containers and packages and safe loading and unloading procedures. They require accident reports and remedial action as well as more routine record keeping and reporting. The DOT conducts inspections to monitor compliance. NOTE: Other RSPA regulations cover pipeline gas. 49 C.F.R. Part 190 *et seq.*

For example, the familiar red diamond-shaped placards on trucks and red labels on 55-gallon steel drums and other containers indicating flammability are required by RSPA's regulations. RSPA's regulations are enforced by other DOT administrations for shipments by the rail, air, water and motor vehicle carriers which they regulate, i.e., the Federal Railway Administration (FRA), the Federal Aviation Administration (FAA), the U.S. Coast Guard (USCG) and the Federal Highway Administration (FHWA). Each administration has adopted implementing regulations. RSPA regulates intermodal shipments.

Effective October 1, 1990, the DOT adopted a comprehensive new rule, known as HM-181, restructuring its regulations for packaging and transporting hazardous materials. The rules are being phased in gradually over several years and full compliance is scheduled for 1996. Among other objectives, the rules were intended to align U.S. rules with those of other United Nations member countries and thus avoid dual markings for domestic and international packaging.

HM-181 made fundamental changes in testing, classification, packaging, labelling and shipping document requirements. For example, the 22 classes of materials used by DOT became 9 classes based on chemical reactions. New packaging standards were performance-based rather than specification-based. Warning labels and placards correspond to those prescribed in the United Nations Convention on the Transport of Dangerous Goods. The new rules required extensive training and retraining of employees.

In November 1990, Congress enacted the Hazardous Materials Transportation Uniform Safety Act (HMTUSA), 49 U.S.C. App. § 5101 *et seq.*, which, among other things, made changes to the HMTA limiting the authority of states to pass legislation unless it is substantially the same as federal rules governing the marking, labeling, packaging, placarding and classification of hazardous materials for transport. See *Chlorine Institute v. Cal. Highway Patrol*, 29 F. 3d 495 (9th Cir. 1994). Under the HMTUSA, highway routing is an area of joint federal and state jurisdiction. The HMTUSA authorizes grants to states to be used to develop emergency response programs, for spills and releases, and to train public sector employees to respond properly to an emergency. In November 1990, Congress also enacted the Sanitary Food Transportation Act of 1990 (SFTA), 49 U.S.C. App. § 2801 *et seq.* Section 15 of the SFTA contains the Motor Carrier Safety Act of 1990 (MCSA).

By legislation signed by the President on August 26, 1994, the HMTA was reauthorized through the federal government's 1997 fiscal year. Modest amendments were included in the legislation including an exemption of foreign offerers from U.S. registration fees.

XIV. MARINE PROTECTION, RESEARCH AND SANCTU-ARIES ACT

The Marine Protection, Research and Sanctuaries Act (MPRSA), 33 U.S.C. § 1401 *et seq.*, prohibits ocean dumping of radiological, chemical and biological warfare agents, high level radioactive wastes and medical wastes. The MPRSA requires a permit from the USEPA for ocean dumping of other substances. As administered by the USEPA, it is difficult to obtain a permit. The U.S. Army Corps of Engineers is authorized to issue permits to transport dredged materials for ocean disposal at sites including those designated by the USEPA after EIS procedures. The U.S. Coast Guard joins in enforcement of the MPRSA by detecting violations.

The USEPA's regulations are at 40 C.F.R. Part 220 *et seq.* Regulations relating to the evaluation of dredge and fill permits by the Corps of Engineers are at 40 C.F.R. Part 225.

Under existing amendments and enforcement policies, no ocean dumping of industrial waste is permitted except in emergencies. Ocean dumping of sewage sludge is also not permitted. Because of strong political opposition, permits for ocean incineration are also denied by the USEPA except for research.

XV. OCCUPATIONAL SAFETY AND HEALTH ACT

A. General

The Occupational Safety and Health Act (the "OSH Act"), 29 U.S.C. § 651 *et seq.*, created the Occupational Safety and Health Administration (OSHA) within the U.S. Department of Labor and established programs for the protection of safety and health in the nation's workplaces. The OSH Act also established the National Institute for Occupational Safety and Health (NIOSH) to conduct research and experimental programs.

Major programs include adoption of safety and health standards; research programs including ways to discover latent diseases and work-related causes; hazard communication regulations requiring preparation of material safety data sheets (MSDS) and that employers assemble and make available to workers and their representatives information about hazardous materials used in the workplace; and nationwide inspections of workplaces to detect violations. The OSH Act requires each employer to furnish employment and a workplace free from recognized hazards causing or likely to cause death or serious physical harm. Both employers and employees must comply with the standards and the rules, regulations and orders of OSHA.

OSHA has adopted extensive regulations under the Act. 29 C.F.R. Part 1900 *et seq.* They include review and approval of state plans; inspections, citations and penalties; recording and reporting of occupational injuries and illnesses; accreditation of testing laboratories; and safety and health standards. An index to the numerous safety and health standards is provided following 29 C.F.R. § 1910.1500.

B.   National Consensus Standards

National consensus standards on safety and health were adopted by OSHA shortly after the Act became effective based on existing standards of other government agencies and industry organizations. A list of standards incorporated by reference to standards of ANSI, ASTM, NFPA and other industry organizations is provided at the end of 29 C.F.R. § 1910.1500.

C.   Safety Standards

Safety standards adopted by OSHA are numerous and detailed. They include design and performance specifications for equipment used in the workplace such as machinery, tools, electrical systems, compressed gases, vehicles, and personal protective equipment worn by workers.

D.   Health Standards

Health standards have been more difficult to adopt and sustain, especially for substances having potential long term effects. OSHA's health standards have sometimes been challenged in court based on questions about new toxicological methods used by OSHA. However, a contributing factor to these challenges is the OSHA tradition that workers are entitled to standards that apply to the workplaces of small and medium-sized businesses as well as those of large corporations with extensive resources. OSHA's broad inspection and enforcement policy benefits workers who most need protection. However, it results in active opposition to its regulations by some small and medium-sized businesses who know that OSHA will require them to comply and fear the cost and difficulty of doing so.

E.   Air Contaminants Standard

On January 19, 1989, OSHA adopted and published at 54 Fed. Reg. 2,332 a final rule revising and greatly expanding its Air Contaminants Standard to establish permissible exposure limits for several hundred hazardous substances. The standards include short term exposure limits as well as 8 hour time weighted average limits. However, the revised Air Contaminants Standard was vacated by court order in *AFL v. OSHA, 965 F.2d 962 (11th Cir. 1992)*. Many businesses have chosen to comply with the standards voluntarily. OSHA is currently considering proposals to establish new exposure limits for smaller numbers of hazardous substances.

F.   Chemical Process Standard

In 1992, OSHA adopted a major standard for the management of the hazards of processes using specified highly hazardous chemicals. This innovative process standard was mandated by Section 304 of the Clean Air Act Amendments of 1990 to reduce the threat of accidental releases of chemicals in the workplace. The standard recognizes that chemical processes are continually changing in response to technology and, therefore, places responsibility on the employer to make detailed written analyses of hazards involved in their processes and to adopt operating procedures, employee training, emergency response plans, pre-startup review procedures, mechanical integrity inspection procedures, hot work permits, incident investigation procedures and compliance audits. The written procedures must include management of change so that changes of chemicals, equipment and other elements are evaluated for their effects on the whole process. The standard also provides for access to information and participation by employees and their representatives, typically a labor union. 29 C.F.R. § 1910.119.

G.   Hazardous Waste Operations.

In 1989, OSHA adopted regulations governing hazardous waste and emergency response operations, commonly called the "HAZWOPER." 29 C.F.R. § 1910.120. The HAZWOPER applies to cleanup operations at uncontrolled hazardous waste sites under CERCLA and state law programs; corrective actions at TSD facilities under RCRA; and emergency response operations involving hazardous substances regardless of location. OSHA's HAZWOPER requires that employers establish a written safety and health program and take other steps including site characterization and analysis; site control; training of management, supervisors and workers; medical surveillance; establishment of engineering control, work practice and personal protective equipment programs; air monitoring; information programs; container handling procedures; decontamination procedures; emergency response plans; sanitation facilities; new technology programs; and other special programs. Illinois licensing legislation regulating worker safety and health was pre-empted by the OSH Act and the HAZWOPER regulations. *Gade v. National Solid Wastes*, 505 U.S.--, 120 L. Ed. 2d 73, (1992)

H.   Bloodborne Pathogens Standard

In 1992, OSHA also adopted a bloodborne pathogens standard limiting occupational exposure to blood and other potentially infectious materials. The standard was developed in response to highly publicized incidents involving alleged transmission of the HIV virus and Hepatitis B in hospitals and in medical and dental offices. However, OSHA did not restrict the standard to the health care industry. It applies to any employer whose employees are occupationally exposed to blood or other potentially infectious materials. The extensive and detailed requirements of the standard have initially been difficult for individual doctors, dentists and other small employers to implement. 29 C.F.R. § 1910.1030.

I.   Penalties

For many years, OSHA followed a policy of imposing relatively modest fines for violations if corrective actions were taken.

The fines took into account the ability of small businesses, which commit the most numerous and serious violations, to pay the fines without impairing their ability to do business. To be consistent, OSHA fined large businesses by the same standards. Recently, faced with amendments to the OSH Act and political criticism, OSHA has imposed larger fines. These fines are a controversial area of OSHA's enforcement strategy because they impose high amount, high-publicity citations for what the agency calls "egregious willful" violations. Since the beginning of 1989, OSHA has proposed that a number of penalties totalling over a million dollars be imposed on employers. In 1994, OSHA proposed penalties of several million dollars for some employers. OSHA defines willful as intentional disregard or plain indifference to the employer's responsibility. OSHA does not define "egregious willful" but has applied the term where it believes employers have flagrantly disregarded their responsibilities under the OSH Act. The common element in all such citations is the fact that the alleged wrong affected a large number of employees, such as a substantial under-recording of occupational illnesses and injuries, failure to train employees in dangerous occupations, or failure to provide required respiratory protection.

J.   State Administration

The OSH Act authorizes states to assume responsibility for occupational health and safety and health standards by submitting a plan, including necessary laws and regulations, for approval by OSHA. 29 C.F.R. Part 1901 *et seq*. The state plan must be at least as effective as the standards adopted by OSHA. Only about half of the states have done so. Those states which have not acted are preempted from adopting such safety and health standards. However, the preemption does not prevent the enforcement of state criminal laws for conduct which violates OSHA health and safety standards.

K.   The Role of OSHA

OSHA has extensive practical experience which exceeds that of recently created environmental agencies. Only the DOT has a corresponding experience. OSHA has traditionally resisted efforts to use its enforcement powers as a tool in collective bargaining. The result has sometimes been criticism by persons who wanted OSHA to adopt their viewpoint rather than to reach its own determination. However, OSHA's relative independence has helped it to develop effective programs which have contributed to the dramatic decline of work - related deaths since 1970 as reported by the National Safety Council.

XVI. LAWS RELATING TO LEAD

Since the days of the Athenian and Roman Empires, lead has been known as a useful and versatile metal, but also as a hazardous substance when misused. During this century, lead and lead compounds have been widely used in batteries, electronic circuit boards, paint driers and pigments, cable sheathing, piping, solder, radiation shielding, printer's type, ammunition, glass, sporting equipment and tetraethyl lead gasoline additives.

During the last three decades, environmental and safety groups in the U.S. have sponsored numerous laws restricting products containing lead and lead compounds. The most important laws have restricted lead in motor vehicle fuels, water pipes and solder, and paints and coatings. New laws have also restricted lead emitted by industries manufacturing or using lead or lead compounds.

In recent decades, the blood lead levels in the United States have declined sharply. See the EPA's advance notice of proposed rule making, 56 Fed. Reg. 20,096 (5/13/91) and the *Journal of the American Medical Association*, Vol. 272, No. 4, July 1994 and No. 6, August 1994. Symptomatic cases of lead poisoning are rare in the U.S. Nevertheless, federally-funded research teams at the U.S. Centers for Disease Control have repeatedly issued reports reducing safety criteria levels and warning the public of an epidemic of lead poisoning affecting children and emphasizing the need for further research. The result is continuing enactment of new laws and regulations including major programs to warn the public about lead and to require removal or remediation of lead-containing paint, pipe and other products.

A brief summary of the major laws and regulations governing lead and lead compounds is as follows:

A. Clean Air Act

EPA regulations under the CAA establish national ambient air quality standards (NAAQS) for lead as particulate matter, i.e. 150 ug/m, 24 hour average concentration (PM10) and 50 ug/m, annual arithmetic mean (PM10). 40 CFR § 50.6. They also establish an air quality standard for lead itself of 1.5 ug/cm, maximum arithmetic mean, quarterly average.

EPA regulations establish national emission standards for industrial processes which emit lead to the atmosphere, such as primary lead smelters. 40 CFR § 60.180.

The Act has for several years restricted manufacture and sale of vehicle fuels containing lead. Leaded gasoline cannot be sold for motor vehicle use after December 31, 1995.

B. Clean Water Act

EPA regulations under the CWA establish reportable quantities for spills of lead and lead compounds. 40 CFR § 117.3. Lead compounds are included in the list of hazardous substances. 40 CFR § 116.4.

Discharges of lead and lead compounds are among those governed by the national pollutant discharge elimination system. (40 CFR part 122); the state water quality standards regulations (40 CFR Part 131); the effluent guidelines and standards (40 CFR Part 401-471); and the sewage sludge management regulations (40 CFR § 503.13).

C. Safe Drinking Water Act

EPA regulations under SDWA set a maximum contaminant level goal (MCLG) of zero for lead in drinking water. 40 CFR § 141.51. They also require community water systems to install and operate corrosion control equipment to minimize lead concentration in drinking water. Any community water system exceeding an action level of 0.015 mg/L must also meet source water treatment, lead service line replacement and public education requirements. 40 CFR § 141.80 *et seq.* However, the regulations were partially vacated in *American Water Works Ass'n v. EPA*, No. 91-1338, 1994 U.S. App. LEXIS 34174 (D.C. Cir., Dec. 6, 1994). Drinking water pipe containing more than 8% lead and solder and flux containing more than 0.2% lead are prohibited. 42 U.S.C. §§ 300g-6 and 300j-24.

D.   Resource Conservation and Recovery Act

EPA's regulations under RCRA establish criteria for municipal solid waste landfills list lead and lead compounds in their groundwater standards, design criteria for landfills, and list of hazardous constituents. 40 CFR Parts 257 and 258. Certain specific wastes containing lead or lead compounds are among those included in the hazardous waste lists in 40 CFR § 261.30 to 33. Wastes containing lead or lead compounds may also be hazardous wastes if they do not meet toxic characteristic leaching procedure (TCLP) tests prescribed in 40 CFR § 261.24.

E.   CERCLA

EPA regulations establish reportable quantities for lead and lead compounds. 40 CFR, Table 302.4. EPA soil lead guidance for CERCLA Sites recommends a screening level of 400 ppm for land used for residential purposes. However, the guidance refers to TSCA guidelines for soil cleanup in the range of 400 to 5,000 ppm and soil amendment in excess of 5,000 ppm. OSWER Directive 9355.4-12.

F.   Occupational Safety and Health Act

OSHA's regulations include a general industry standard and a construction industry standard for lead exposure in the workplace. 29 C.F.R. §§ 1910.1025 and 1926.62. In both standards, the personnel exposure limit (PEL) is 50 ug/m, 8 hour TWA and the action level is 30 ug/m 8 hour TWA. Lead and lead compounds are among the materials covered by the hazard communication rules. 29 CFR § 1910.1200, Appendix A. OSHA, now headed by Robert Reich, a former professor at Harvard University, has proposed some of the largest fines ever imposed by OSHA for alleged violations of the new construction industry standard by small firms engaged in bridge painting, i.e., $3.7 million in *Reich v. Manganas Paint Co.* and $6.0 million in *Reich v. E. Smalis Painting Co.*

G.   Consumer Product Safety Act

The Consumer Product Safety Act, 15 U.S.C., § 2501 *et seq.* bans the sale of lead-containing paint, i.e., lead content in excess of 0.06% by weight of nonvolatile content or dried film, unless exempted. The ban also includes articles (such as toys or furniture) bearing lead-containing paint. 16 CFR Part 1303.

H.   Toxic Substances Control Act

Numerous tasks relating to lead-based paint were assigned to the EPA by amendments to TSCA enacted in 1992. TSCA defines lead-based paint as containing greater than 1.0 mg/cm or 0.5% by weight.

Among other steps, the U.S. EPA has issued booklets on home remodelling and protection of children. The U.S. EPA has announced grants to nonprofit organizations to train abatement workers and grants to states for accreditation and certification for professionals. The U.S. EPA has issued interim cleanup guidance for residential lead-based paint, lead-contaminated dust, and lead-contaminated soil. OPPTS 9355.4-15, 7/14/94. The U.S. EPA has also issued a proposed rule governing lead-based activities, i.e., accreditation of training programs, certification of individuals and firms, standards for conducting activities, and requirement that activities be conducted only according to the prescribed procedures and standards and by certified individuals or firms. 59 Fed. Reg. 45872, 9/2/94.

TSCA also requires the U.S. EPA to issue regulations to become effective October 28, 1995 requiring that every seller and lessor of "target housing" meet several requirements for the benefit of the buyer or tenant. "Target housing" means any housing constructed prior to 1978 except certain housing for the elderly and disabled. The requirements are to furnish a lead hazard information pamphlet prepared by the EPA, disclose the presence of any known lead-based paint or hazards in the housing, and permit a 10-day period to conduct a risk assessment or inspection. Contracts for purchase or sale of any interest in target housing must contain a warning statement and a statement signed by the purchaser that evidences compliance with the requirements of TSCA. The U.S. EPA and HUD proposed joint regulations to implement the notification requirements are found at 59 Fed. Reg. 54,984, 11/2/94.

I. Lead-Based Paint Poisoning Prevention Act, 42 U.S.C. § 4801 and the Residential Lead-Based Paint Reduction Act, 42 U.S.C.§ 4851.

These Acts provide for a wide variety of programs including amendments to the laws previously described. In addition, they provide for major programs of the Department of Housing and Urban Development (HUD) which govern the identification and abatement of lead-based paint in federally assisted housing and are found in many parts of 24 C.F.R.

In April, 1990, HUD published Interim Guidelines for hazard identification and abatement of lead-based paint in Public and Indian Housing Programs assisted under the Comprehensive Improvement Assistance Program (CIAP), 55 Fed. Reg. 14,556 (4/18/90). The Interim Guidelines contain extensive requirements and also valuable information about methods and technologies.

HUD presented a Report to Congress dated December 7, 1990 of a Comprehensive and Workable Plan for the Abatement of Lead-Based Paint in Privately Owned Housing in response to 1987 amendments to the LBPPPA. In 1991, HUD issued The HUD Lead-Based Paint Abatement Demonstration (FHA), August, 1991, reporting on multi-city abatement projects which it had sponsored. These reports contain extensive information for those interested in the hazards and abatement of lead-based paint.

HUD is also authorized to provide grants for studies and for rehabilitation of federally financed and subsidized housing under several laws including the National Housing Act (42 U.S.C. § 1441 *et seq.*) and the Housing and Community Development Act (42 U.S.C. § 5301 *et seq.*). These laws have perennially been amended and expanded by legislation such as the McKinney Homeless Assistance Amendments Act of 1988, the Cranston-Gonzalez National Affordable Housing Act of 1990, and the Housing and Community Development Act Amendments of 1992. Among the grant programs are Section 8 Grants, Community Development Block Grants and HOME Grants.

In May 1994, HUD proposed to amend its regulations to reduce childhood age to 6 years of age; establish the intervention standard at 20 ug/dl (one test) or 15-19 ug/dl (two tests several months apart); define lead-based paint as 1.0 mg/cm determined by X-ray fluorescence analyzer or laboratory analysis with 0.5% by weight (5,000 ppm) as an alternative; and generally to update the rules applicable to lead-based paint in federally subsidized housing including methods for inspection, sampling, testing, abatement and cleanup. 59 Fed. Reg. 24850, May 12, 1994.

J.   State Environmental and Health Laws

The states have adopted environmental laws implementing the federal environmental laws including the CAA, CWA, SWDA, RCRA and CERCLA. Many states also adopted health laws to regulate lead-based paint hazards. Some of these laws have established only limited programs. Others provide for comprehensive programs which may be found in the laws and in the implementing regulations adopted by applicable health, environmental, and housing agencies. In general, the more comprehensive laws and regulations are found in the northeastern states.

Examples of the provisions of the comprehensive programs are screening of children; mandatory reports of "lead poisoning" as defined in terms of micrograms per deciliter (ug/dl) of blood; inspection and evaluation of residences for lead-based paint as defined in terms of lead content by weight or per square centimeter; abatement of lead-based paint hazards as specified; notice to a designated agency prior to abatement work; licensing and training of abatement contractors and personnel; prohibition of retaliation by owners against tenants; and imposition of strict liability on owners under some circumstances.

The regulations in states such as Massachusetts and Maryland are quite detailed, particularly as to the methods, equipment and performance standards for abatement. For example, abatement rules often prescribe inspection methods and equipment (x-ray fluorescence analyzer, atomic absorption analyzer, or sodium sulfide); occupant and property removal or protection; methods for containment of the work area with polyethylene sheeting and sealants; warnings and restriction of access to the work area; the surface which must be abated; prohibited abatement methods; permitted abatement methods; cover materials useable for encapsulation; worker protection during abatement; cleanup requirements such as HEPA filters; reoccupancy inspection requirements; lead dust levels during and at the end of abatement work; disposal of wastes; record keeping; and issuance of certificates of compliance.

K.   Lead-Based Paint Litigation

Lawsuits have been commenced against large paint manufacturers which were members of the Lead Industries Association seeking to impose alternative, enterprise or market share liability. Recent decisions in favor of defendants indicate that these efforts may generally be unsuccessful. *City of Philadelphia v. Lead Industries Association, Inc.*, 994 F.2d 112 (3d Cir. 1993); *Santiago v. Sherwin-Williams Company*, 782 F. Supp. 186 (D. Mass. 1993), affirmed 3 F.3d 546 (1st Cir. 1993); *Setiff v. E.1. du. Pont et al.* No. CO 17713 (Cal. App. 3d Dist. 1995; but see *City of New York v. Lead Industries Association, Inc.*, 597 N.Y.S. 2d 698 (1st Dept. 1993).

Many lawsuits are being commenced against landlords with various results. *Bencosme v. Kokoras*, 400 Mass. 40, 507 N.E. 2d 748 (1987); *Hardy v. Griffin*, 41 Conn. Sup. 283, 569 A.2d 49 (1989); *Underwood v. Risman*, 605 N.E. 2d 832 (Mass. 1993); *Hill v. City of New York*, 201 A.D. 2d 329 (1st Dept. 1994); *Holmes by Holloway v. City of New York*, 592 N.Y. S. 2d 371 (1st Dept. 1993); *Brown v. Marathon Realty, Inc.*, 170 A.D. 2d 426, 565 N.Y.S. 2d 219 (2d Dept. 1991); *Miller v. Beaugrand*, 169 A.D. 2nd 537, 564 N.Y.S. 2d 390

(1st Dept. 1991); *Winston Properties v. Sanders*, 565 N.E. 2d 1280 (Ohio App. 1989); *Garcia v. Jimenez*, 184 Ill. App. 35 107 (2d Dist. 1989).

Many lawsuits are being commenced against insurers seeking defense and indemnification against liability or to recover abatement costs under general liability policies. *U.S. Liability v. Bourbeau*, —F. 3d— (1st Cir. 1995); St. Leger v. American Fire, 870 F. Supp. (E.D. Pa. 1994); *NL Industries v. Commercial Union*, 828 F. Supp. 1154 ((D. N.J. 1993); *Sherwin-Williams v. Lloyds*, 813F. Supp. 576 (N.D. Ohio 1993); *Scottsdale Insurance v. American Surplus*, 811 F. Supp. 210 (D. Md. 1993); *Generali-U.S. Branch v.Caribe Realty*, 612 N.Y.S. 2d 296 (N.Y. City, 1994); *Schumann v. State*, 610 N.Y.S. 2d 987 (Ct. Cl. 1994); Oates v. State of New York, 597 N.Y.S. 2d 550 (Ct. Claims, 1993); J.A.M. Associates v. Western World Insurance Co., 622 A.2d 818 (Md. App. 1993); Harford County v. Harford Mutual Insurance Co., 327 Md. 418, 610 A.2d 286 (1992); Atlantic Mutual Insurance Company v. McFadden, 413 Mass. 90, 595 N.E. 2d 762 (Mass. 1992).

XVII. THE OIL POLLUTION ACT

The Oil Pollution Act (OPA) was adopted in 1990 as a reaction to the oil spill which resulted when the Exxon Valdez ran aground in Prince William Sound off the shore of Alaska. Many of the provisions are found at 33 U.S.C. § 2701 *et seq.*, including the Great Lakes Oil Pollution Research and Development Act which begins at 33 U.S.C. § 2761 *et seq.* However, the OPA also included amendments to the Clean Water Act, 33 U.S.C. § 2701 *et seq.* and the Trans-Alaska Pipeline System Act, 43 U.S.C. § 1651 *et seq.*

A. Liability Provisions

The OPA provides that each responsible party for a vessel or facility from which oil is discharged, or which poses a substantial threat of an oil discharge, into navigable waters of the United States, the adjoining shorelines, or the exclusive economic zone claimed by the United States by Presidential Proclamation and treaties is liable for removal costs and damages. The liability is imposed upon each responsible party, thus making it likely that the liability is joint and several. The liability is also imposed notwithstanding any other provision or rule of law. 33 U.S.C. § 2702(a).

Removal costs incurred by the U.S., a state, or an Indian Tribe under certain sections of the CWA, the Intervention on the High Seas Act or state law can be recovered by those governmental organizations. Removal costs can also be recovered by other persons for acts taken in compliance with the National Contingency Plan. Specified claimants can recover damages for injury to, destruction of, loss of, or loss of use of, natural resources and real or personal property. Recovery is also authorized for loss of subsistence use of natural resources, lost revenues, lost profits and earning capacity, and net costs of providing additional public services. 33 U.S.C. § 2702(b).

The liability does not apply to any discharge permitted by a permit issued under federal, state or local law. It also does not apply to a discharge from a vessel owned or bareboat chartered and operated by the U.S., a state or political subdivision thereof, or a foreign nation, except when the vessel is engaged in commerce. 33 U.S.C. § 2702(e).

The OPA defines a "vessel" to include every description of watercraft other than a public vessel. Thus, its application goes beyond large tanker vessels to include the working vessels of private businesses and recreational vessels owned by private citizens. The OPA also defines a "facility" extremely broadly to include even motor vehicles.

The OPA defines a responsible party for a vessel as any person owning, operating or demise chartering the vessel. The OPA defines a responsible party for an onshore facility and an offshore facility so as to include any person who is an owner or operator except governmental entities. 33 U.S.C. § 2701(32).

If a third party is *solely* responsible, the OPA requires that the responsible party pay the removal costs and damages and then sue the third party based on the rights of the U.S. and the claimants paid. The OPA contains narrow "innocent purchaser" defenses similar to those contained in CERCLA. 33 U.S.C. §§ 2702(d) and 2703. The

OPA contains limits on liability, but the amounts are very high. 33 U.S.C. § 2704.

The OPA contains two provisions of which provide some modest relief to private businesses and private citizens. Contribution actions against other persons who are or may be liable are authorized by 33 U.S.C. § 2709. Indemnification agreements are authorized by 33 U.S.C. § 2710.

B. Financial Responsibility

The OPA imposes extensive financial responsibility requirements on owners and operators of vessels, offshore facilities and deepwater ports. 33 U.S.C. §§ 2716 and 2716a. The requirements apply to the responsible party for (1) any vessel over 300 gross tons except a non-self-propelled vessel (barge) that does not carry oil as cargo or fuel and (2) any vessel using the waters of the exclusive economic zone to tranship or lighter oil destined for a place subject to U.S. jurisdiction, 33 U.S.C. § 2716(a).

Each responsible party must provide to the Coast Guard evidence of financial responsibility sufficient to meet its maximum amount of OPA liability. However, a responsible party for more than one vessel need only meet the maximum liability of its vessel having the greatest maximum liability.

The OPA provides that financial responsibility may be established by any one or combination of the following methods which the Coast Guard for vessels and the USEPA for facilities determine to be acceptable: insurance, surety bond, guarantee, letter of credit, qualification as a self-insurer, or other evidence. The OPA limits the defenses available to a guarantor of the financial responsibility of a responsible party. 33 U.S.C. § 2716(e). However, it allows a guarantor to establish an aggregate limit with respect to an incident on the amount of financial responsibility provided to a responsible party. 33 U.S.C. § 2716(g).

On December 10, 1993, the National Petroleum Council issued a report saying that the financial responsibility requirements may have a severe adverse effect on small oil and gas producers who drill offshore.

C.   The Oil Spill Liability Fund

The OPA contains provisions implementing the Oil Spill Liability Trust Fund created by Section 9509 of the Internal Revenue Code of 1986 (IRC, 1986) by providing provisions for uses of the Fund, claims procedures and related provisions. The Fund derives revenues from an excise tax on of $.05 per barrel on oil received at U.S. refineries and other petroleum products and funds transferred from other sources. The IRC, 1986 imposes a limit of $1.0 billion per incident on government and private uses of, and claims against, the Fund.

D.   Prevention of Oil Pollution

Title IV of the OPA contains numerous provisions intended to prevent oil pollution. Many of them consist of amendments to Title 46 of the U.S. Code. They include stricter standards and procedures for the issuance and renewal of licenses, certificates of registry and merchant mariners' documents and their suspension or revocation for alcohol or drug abuse. The Coast Guard is required to implement stricter manning standards for tank vessels and to evaluate the adequacy of standards of foreign countries for foreign tank vessels. The Coast Guard is required to establish minimum plating thickness standards for bulk oil cargo vessels and to require periodic gauging of the plating thickness of such vessels when over 30 years old. With certain exceptions, new tank vessels must be double hulled. With certain exceptions, tank vessels of at least 5,000 gross tons without a double hull will be phased out over a 20 year period from 1995 to 2015. The Coast Guard is required to issue minimum standards for overfill devices and tank level or pressure monitoring devices.

Some of the provisions in Title IV appear to be motivated at least partially to favor domestic ships and maritime professionals. For example, certain single hulled foreign vessels over 5,000 tons must be escorted in Northwestern waters by two tugs. Certain vessels must use a U.S. or Canadian pilot on the Great Lakes. Certain vessels are required to have a licensed master or mate on the bridge in addition to the pilot.

E.   Removal of Oil Discharges

Title IV of the OPA establishes primary authority of the federal government over the mitigation or prevention of oil discharges and the removal of oil discharges which occur. However, state laws are not preempted. Removal must be accomplished in accordance with the USEPA's National Oil and Hazardous Substances Pollution Contingency Plan (NCP) at 40 C.F.R. § 302. In order to encourage cooperation, the OPA provides that a person is not liable for removal costs or damages which result from actions taken or omitted in the course of rendering care, assistance or advice consistent with the NCP. 42 U.S.C. § 1321.

F.   Regulations

The USEPA, the Coast Guard and other federal government agencies have adopted numerous regulations relating to oil pollution before and after the OPA was enacted. Of special interest are the Coast Guard regulations at 33 C.F.R. Parts 151-158 and the USEPA regulations at 40 C.F.R. Parts 110-112. These regulations coordinate the requirements of the OPA and related laws with the International Convention for the Prevention of Pollution from Ships, 1973, as modified by the Protocol of 1978 done at London on February 17, 1978 (MARPOL 73/78). See also amendments to the CERCLA National Contingency Plan. 59 Fed. Reg. 47384, 9/15/95.

XVIII. LAWS PROTECTING WILDLIFE, FISH, PLANTS & MARINE MAMMALS

A.   The Endangered Species Act.

The Endangered Species Act, 16 U.S.C. § 4321 *et seq.*, contains a number of programs. The most fundamental is its prohibition of various actions including the import, export, possession, sale or "taking" of endangered species of fish, wildlife and plants.

The Act is administered by the Fish & Wildlife Service of the U.S. Department of the Interior (FWS). FWS's regulations are found at 50 C.F.R. Part 10 *et seq.* The Act contains many exceptions, exemptions and authorizations for the issuance of permits by the FWS.

The Act was adopted with widespread public support after extensive campaigns by environmental groups to protect animals such as golden eagles, whooping cranes and buffaloes.

However, the Act defines an endangered species as any species in danger of extinction, except insect pests found by the FWS to present an overwhelming and overriding risk to man. Thus, the FWS has adopted regulations protecting numerous predatory animals such as timber wolves, reptiles and grizzly bears. See, e.g., *Christy v. Hodel* 857 F.2d 1324 (9th Cir. 1988) upholding a fine imposed on a sheep farmer for killing a grizzly bear. The regulations also protect numerous subspecies such as the Indiana bat, the Alabama beach mouse, the Fresno kangaroo rat, several subspecies of darter fish, the Houston toad and the Northern spotted owl. See, e.g. *TVA v. Hill,* 437 U.S. 153 (1978).

The Act states that "take" means to harass, harm, pursue, hunt, shoot, wound, kill, trap, capture or collect, or to attempt to engage in any such conduct. 16 U.S.C. § 1532(19). The FWS adopted regulations much expanding the definition in 50 C.F.R., § 17.3 including even a significant habitat modification resulting in certain adverse effects. This last definition was declared invalid in *Sweet Home Chapter v. Babbitt,* 17 F.3d 1463 (D.C. Cir. 1994), but the U. S. Supreme Court reversed and upheld the expanded definition_____U.S._____ (1995).

The Act requires that the FWS establish a "critical habitat" for each endangered and threatened species that shall not include the entire area that the species could occupy unless otherwise determined by the FWS. The Act directs the FWS to base its designations on the best available scientific evidence after considering economic and other relevant factors and authorizes the FWS to exclude any area from critical habitat. The FWS is authorized to adopt regulations to provide for conservation of threatened as well as endangered species.

16 U.S.C. § 1533. The FWS has designated large areas of the United States as critical habitat. 50 C.F.R. § 17.94 *et seq.*

Environmental groups have successfully sued the FWS when it failed to take action which they believed to be adequate. *Northern Spotted Owl v. Lujan,* 758 F. Supp. 621 (W.D. Wash. 1991.). The Act has become increasingly controversial as the FWS and environmental groups have applied the law and regulations and the National Environmental Policy Act to restrict mining, logging, manufacturing, land development and other industrial, commercial and residential activities. See, e.g., *National Audubon Society v. Espy,* 998 F.2d 699 (9th Cir. 1993). See also later proceedings in the same case considered under several national forest laws including the National Forest Management Act, 16 U.S.C. § 1600 *et seq.* and the Federal Land Policy and Management Act, 43 U.S.C. § 1701 *et seq.,* 871 F. Supp. 1291 (W.D. Wash. 1994).

The U.S. is a party to the Convention on International Trade in Endangered Species which is implemented by 16 U.S.C. § 1537 and the FWS regulations at 50 C.F.R. Part 23.

B.   The Marine Mammal Protection Act

The Marine Mammal Protection Act, 16 U.S.C. § 1361 *et seq.* contains a number of programs. The most fundamental is its prohibition against the "taking" of any marine mammal by persons or in places subject to the jurisdiction of the U.S. except as provided in the Act. The Act also prohibits other actions including importation, possession, transportation, purchase and sale of marine mammals and products from them except as provided in the Act. The Act is administered primarily by the Marine Mammal Commission (MMC), the National Oceanographic and Atmospheric Administration of the Department of the Interior (NOAA) and the FWS. NOAA's regulations are found at 50 C.F.R. § 204 *et seq.* The FWS's regulations are found at 50 C.F.R. Part 18.

The Act protects marine mammals (such as whales, seals, polar bears, dolphins, wolves and others) and does not require that they be endangered. Some marine mammals are covered by the Act and the Endangered Species Act. The Act contains numerous exceptions and exemptions, including exemptions for Alaskan Natives, and provisions for the grant of permits. NOAA's regulations establishing critical habitats for marine mammals are found at 50 C.F.R. Part 226.

C.   Related Laws

Other federal laws for the protection of fish and wildlife include the Bald and Golden Eagle Protection Act, 16 U.S.C. § 668 *et seq.*; the National Wildlife Refuge System Administration Act, 16 U.S.C. § 668dd *et seq.*; the Migratory Bird Acts, 16 U.S.C. § 701 *et seq.*; the Airborne Hunting Act, 16 U.S.C. § 742j-1; the Black Bass Act, 16 U.S.C. § 851 *et seq.*; the Lacey Act, 18 U.S.C. § 43 *et seq.*; and the Lacey Act Amendments, 16 U.S.C. § 3371 *et seq.* For the most part, the regulations implementing these laws are those of the FWS and NOAA in 50 C.F.R.

XIX. NOISE CONTROL LAWS

There are several federal laws which regulate excessive noise. The program with the broadest application is the OSHA's occupational noise exposure regulation. 29 C.F.R. § 1910.95. Among other things, the regulation imposes permissible noise exposure limits (PNELs) ranging from 115 dbA for exposure of 15 minutes or less to 90 dbA for exposure of eight hours. The regulation establishes an action level at 85 decibels per 8 hour time weighted average (TWA). When the action level is equalled or exceeded, an employer must develop and implement a hearing conservation program including monitoring, employee notification, audiometric testing and furnishing hearing protectors at no cost to employees.

Another program was established by the Noise Control Act which requires the USEPA to adopt regulations setting noise emission standards for certain equipment sold in interstate commerce. 42 U.S.C. § 4901 *et seq.* The USEPA has adopted regulations applicable to rail and motor carrier transportation equipment, motor carrier equipment and construction equipment and regulations for certification of low noise emission equipment. The USEPA has also established noise emission control regulations applicable to medium and heavy trucks and motorcycles. The regulations also prescribe warranty and labelling requirements. 40 C.F.R. § 201 *et seq.*

The Department of Transportation is required to develop and promulgate highway noise level standards. 23 C.F.R. § 109(i). The Federal Highway Administration has adopted the procedures for abatement of highway traffic noise and construction noise. 23 C.F.R. Part 772.

The Federal Aviation Administration (FAA) is required, with certain exceptions, to issue regulations proposed by the USEPA to provide control and abatement of aircraft noise and sonic boom. 49 U.S.C. § 1431. The FAA's responsibilities were extensively supplemented by the Aviation Safety and Noise Abatement Act of 1979 and the Airport Noise and Capacity Act of 1990. 49 U.S.C. § 2101 *et seq* and § 2151 *et seq.* The FAA's regulations are in 14 C.F.R. Part 36, § 91.801 *et seq.*, Part 150 and Part 161.

The Department of Labor is required by the Mine Safety and Health Act, 30 U.S.C. § 801 *et seq*, to develop and implement noise standards for mines. The standard adopted by the Mine Safety and Health Administration (MSHA) is found at 30 C.F.R. § 70.500 *et seq.*

XX. LAWS GOVERNING RADIOACTIVE MATERIALS AND WASTES

Radioactive materials occur naturally throughout the world in the form of heavy elements such as radium, uranium and thorium. To use them, they must be mined, milled, concentrated, enriched and processed to increase their radioactivity level. Prior to 1954, the mining and production of radioactive materials in the United States was primarily for weapons systems used by predecessors of the U.S. Department of Defense (DOD).

In 1954, the U.S. Congress adopted the Atomic Energy Act (AEA) to foster peaceful uses of radioactive material. The Atomic Energy Commission (AEC) was appointed to administer the Act. The AEC sponsored and regulated a wide range of peaceful uses including nuclear fuels to generate electric power and a multitude of medical, pharmaceutical and industrial applications.

The safety record for industrial use of radioactive materials has been far better than the record of other major industrial and governmental operations of similar size and complexity. However, public perception of the hazards of radioactive materials has been affected by their early use in weapons and by political controversy. Thus, laws and regulations governing radioactive materials and wastes have grown greatly in number and detail.

The basis for environmental regulation of radioactive materials and wastes is derived primarily from federal laws including the following:

Atomic Energy Act of 1954 and amendments, 42 U.S.C. § 2011 *et seq.* (AEA)

Energy Reorganization Act of 1974 and amendments, 42 U.S.C. § 5801*et seq.* (ERA)

Energy Policy and Conservation Act of 1975 and amendments, 42 U.S.C. § 2022 and § 7901 *et seq.* (UMTRCA)

Low Level Radioactive Waste Policy Act of 1980, 42 U.S.C. § 2021b-d (LLRWPA)

Nuclear Waste Policy Act of 1982, 42 U.S.C. § 10101 *et seq.* and the 1987 amendments (NWPA)

Omnibus Low Level Radioactive Waste Interstate Compact Act of 1986, 42 U.S.C. § 2021

Energy Policy Act of 1992, 42 U.S.C. § 13201 *et seq.*

The general federal environmental laws also contain provisions applicable to certain radioactive materials and wastes, i.e. the CAA, CWA, SDWA, RCRA, CERCLA and HMTA. However, these laws generally exclude source, special nuclear and byproduct material as defined in the AEA. By policy or preemption, they are also not applied where more specific programs exist under the laws specifically applicable to radioactive materials. On the other hand, the Federal Facilities Compliance Act of 1992, which added several sections to RCRA, requires the DOE to comply with RCRA and other federal and state environmental laws.

Several federal agencies regulate radioactive materials and wastes. The Nuclear Regulatory Commission (NRC), which succeeded to the regulatory responsibilities of the AEC under the Energy Reorganization Act of 1974, regulates its several thousand licensees including nuclear power generating facilities. The Department of Energy (DOE) regulates the many facilities which it owns or operates through contractors or for which has been required to assume responsibility. These facilities include laboratories, nuclear fuel production facilities and weapons production and testing facilities. Examples are the Los Alamos, Idaho, Sandia and Lawrence Livermore national laboratories and the plants at Savannah River, South Carolina; Oak Ridge, Tennessee; Fernald, Ohio; and Hanford, Washington. The DOE is responsible for over 20 sites listed on the NPL maintained by the USEPA under CERCLA. The Department of Defense (DOD) regulates numerous sites related to its use, testing and storage of weapons systems and nuclear fuel for high performance submarines. The USEPA has authority under the AEA and the UMTRCA to adopt standards of general application to radioactive materials and waste as well as authority under the other environmental laws which it administers.

The NRC's regulations are found at 10 C.F.R. Parts 20 to 71. They have gradually developed from radiation protection standards to include increasingly detailed standards for management, disposal and cleanup of radioactive contamination and waste during active operation and upon decommissioning. In 1994, the NRC proposed important amendments to its radiological criteria for decommissioning of licensed facilities. 59 C.F.R. 43200, 8/22/94.

The DOE has issued several regulatory orders. DOE Order 5400.4 applies to CERCLA policies and procedures prescribed by the NCP. DOE Order No. 5400.5 prescribes standards and requirements for radiation protection of the public and the environment. DOE Order No. 5820.2A prescribes radioactive waste management requirements including the performance objectives of the NRC's land disposal regulations at 40 C.F.R. Part 61. Formal DOE regulations include its rules for reimbursement of remedial action costs at active uranium and thorium processing sites. 10 C.F.R. Part 265. They also include its guidelines for the recommendation of sites for nuclear waste repositories. 10 C.F.R. Part 960. The DOE recently proposed a new regulation on radiation protection of the public and the environment to become 10 C.F.R. Part 834.

Under the AEA, the USEPA has adopted a high level radioactive waste rule. 40 C.F.R. Part 191. Under the AEA and UMTRCA, the EPA has adopted health and environmental protection standards for the control and cleanup of uranium and thorium mill tailings at certain inactive sites being remediated by the DOE and for uranium and thorium byproduct materials at certain active sites of NRC licensees. Under the AEA, the EPA staff has drafted, but it has not yet proposed, a Radiation Site Cleanup Regulation to become 40 C.F.R. Part 196. The NRC and the USEPA have said that this Regulation will not apply to NRC licensees if the EPA is satisfied with the adequacy of the NRC's proposed amended decommissioning rules described earlier.

The EPA has adopted under the CAA a national emission standard for emissions to the air of radon and other radionuclides from several specific sources. 40 C.F.R. Part 61. The EPA has adopted maximum contaminant limits under the CWA for certain radionuclides. 40 C.F.R. Part 141. The EPA regulates radioactive wastes under RCRA except for source, special nuclear and byproduct materials defined in the AEA that are not mixed with other wastes (mixed wastes) subject to RCRA. Accordingly, mixed wastes and other radioactive wastes are subject to the USEPA's hazardous waste management system regulations including the "land ban" regulations. 40 C.F.R. Part 261 *et seq.* Radioactive materials are also subject to CERCLA and the USEPA's regulations at 40 C.F.R. Part 300 *et seq.*, except that the definition of a release excludes any release of source, special nuclear and byproduct materials as defined in the AEA.

The DOT has adopted regulations governing transportation of radioactive materials found in various sections of 40 C.F.R. Parts 171-180. The NRC also has regulations applicable to transportation of radioactive materials, including fissile materials, by its licensees. 10 C.R.R. Part 61. The NRC's regulations, among other things, require its licensees to comply with the DOT regulations, even in some circumstances where the DOT's regulations do not apply.

An important matter of national concern is lack of permanent disposal facilities for radioactive wastes, whether described as high level wastes or low level wastes. High level waste includes irradiated reactor fuel, certain liquid wastes from solvent extraction cycles, and solid wastes into which the liquid wastes have been converted. Low level wastes are wastes not classified as high level waste, transuranic waste, spent fuel, or byproduct materials such as uranium and thorium mill tailings.

In 1983, the U.S. Congress adopted the NWPA to sponsor the selection and development of disposal sites for high level radioactive waste. The NWPA originally directed the DOE to recommend five sites to be characterized as permanent disposal sites, but subsequent amendments focussed on the characterization of a site at Yucca Mountain, Nevada. The NWPA also directed the DOE to develop plans for monitored retrievable storage (MRS) sites that would not be permanent disposal sites.

Programs of the DOE to implement the NWPA have been extremely costly and are expected to total $9 billion dollars by 1998 when the DOE is scheduled to complete its characterization of the Yucca Mountain site. They have also met serious and continuing political opposition. The State of Nevada enacted a law prohibiting the storage of high level radioactive waste and commenced litigation against the DOE, but was unsuccessful. *Nevada v. Watkins*, 914 F.2d 1545 (9th Cir. 1990); *Nevada v. Watkins*, 943 F.2d 1080 (9th Cir. 1991). The State of Tennessee also unsuccessfully challenged the DOE's identification of three sites in Tennessee for possible development as MRS sites. *Tennessee v. Herrington*, 806 F.2d 642 (6th Cir. 1986).

Pending licensing of the Yucca Mountain site, the DOE, nuclear power plants and other facilities must rely on temporary storage facilities for high level waste. The problems of the DOE were recently highlighted when it was required to accept 153 spent fuel rods containing enriched uranium from foreign research reactors as part of the nuclear nonproliferation programs.

When the DOE completes the site characterization of the Yucca Mountain site, it must apply to the NRC for a license to dispose of high level waste. The NRC has adopted regulations governing the licensing of the DOE for disposal of high level radioactive wastes in geologic depositories pursuant to the NWPA. 40 C.F.R. Part 60. Among other things, the regulations provide for participation by states and affected Indian Tribes. The NRC has also adopted regulations governing licenses to the DOE and others for an independent spent fuel storage installation and for MRS sites. 40 C.F.R. Part 72.

In 1980, the U.S. Congress adopted the LLRWPA to provide for the selection and development of sites for the disposal of low level radioactive waste. As amended in 1985, the LLRWPA makes the states responsible for disposal of low level radioactive waste generated within their borders. The LLRWPA authorizes the states to enter into regional compacts under which a state may agree to develop a host site for waste from within its own borders and from the other compact member states. It also authorizes compact states to refuse waste from outside the compact regions. Many states have now entered into compacts and the only states with existing disposal sites (Nevada, South Carolina and Washington) are among them. Thus, hospitals, laboratories, universities and industries which generate low level radioactive waste in several states (such as New York) do not have access to any site and must store the waste under temporary arrangements. As a result, most states, supported by LLRWPA incentives, are gradually moving forward with steps toward selection and development of sites. The NRC has adopted regulations governing licenses for land disposal of low level radioactive waste. 40 C.F.R. Part 61. Among other things, they provide for participation by state governments and affected Indian Tribes.

XXI. OTHER FEDERAL ENVIRONMENTAL LAWS

In addition to the major laws described, there are numerous other federal laws which affect the environment. Some of them are as follows:

Consumer Product Safety Act

Federal Food, Drug, and Cosmetic Act

Intervention on the High Seas Act

National Ocean Pollution Planning Act

Outer Continental Shelf Lands Act

Port and Tanker Safety Act

XXII. LIMITATIONS IMPOSED BY THE U.S. CONSTITUTION

The U.S. Supreme Court and the lower federal courts have consistently upheld the constitutionality of the environmental laws when challenged in early lawsuits making broad-based arguments based on potential for interpretation and application of the laws in a manner that would violate the U.S. Constitution.

During the last century, Mr. Dooley, the creation of the famous humorist, Finley Peter Dunne, observed that the Supreme Court reads the election returns. When Congress adopts laws prepared in response to public concerns, the U.S. Supreme Court customarily exercises judicial restraint in early efforts to raise constitutional issues. This technique allows government agencies and the lower courts to implement the laws while using care to interpret and apply them within constitutional principles. Generally, they do so.

As time passes, serious issues inevitably arise. However, most of them can be resolved on narrow grounds. For example, vague wording in a law can be interpreted broadly or narrowly so as to keep the law within constitutional bounds. Improper actions by government agencies can be nullified because of failure to follow their own regulations or by denying enforcement of regulations unauthorized by the law.

Because of these practical judicial techniques, few questions ultimately require constitutional review. Further, such questions tend to arise only after ample opportunity for government agencies and others to implement programs achieving the broad remedial objective of the laws. The passage of time also allows an opportunity to develop experience and evidence useful in deciding how constitutional principles should be applied.

XXII. LIMITATIONS IMPOSED BY THE U.S. CONSTITUTION

In recent years, the Supreme Court has rendered decisions holding that some actions taken because of the environmental laws have exceeded constitutional bounds. In 1992, the Supreme Court held that an additional fee of $72 per ton imposed by the State of Alabama on hazardous waste disposed of at a licensed privately-owned site at Emelle, Alabama was invalid because it constituted an impermissible burden on interstate commerce in violation of the U.S. Constitution. *Chemical Waste Management, Inc. v. Hunt*, 119 L.Ed.2d 121 (1992); See also *Oregon Waste Systems v. Oregon Dept. of Environmental Liability*, No. 93-70, 1994 U.S. LEXIS 2659 (4/4/94). Provisions of the Illinois Clean Coal Act encouraging the installation of stack emission scrubbing equipment in order to allow public utilities to purchase high-sulfur coal mined in Illinois over low-sulfur coal mined in western states were also held to discriminate impermissibly against interstate commerce. *Alliance for Clean Coal v. Miller*, 44 F.3d 591 (7th Cir. 1994).

In 1992 and 1994, the Supreme Court held that "waste flow" laws and regulations adopted in Michigan and New York were invalid because they discriminated against out-of-state waste in violation of the U.S. Constitution. *Fort Gratiot Sanitary Landfill v. Michigan Dept. of Natural Resources*. 112 S. Ct. 2019 (1992); *C&A Carbone, Inc. v. Town of Clarkstown*, 114 S. Ct. 1677 (1994). The "waste flow" laws presented a difficult question. They were adopted by many states to encourage municipalities to construct waste treatment and disposal facilities. To encourage confidence among investors purchasing bonds to finance the facilities, state legislatures adopted "waste flow" laws granting franchise monopolies to each municipal facility for all waste generated in its district and prohibiting each from accepting waste from generations outside the district. However, the benefit of having local waste treatment and disposal facilities was sometimes lost by inefficient high cost operations and a tendency to impose much higher fees on private industry than on local residents. Industrial waste generators and long distance trucking companies challenged the "waste flow" laws and did so successfully in the *Fort Gratiot* and *C&A, Carbone* cases. Currently, the U.S. Congress is considering legislation which might partially restore the "waste flow" laws to protect at least existing municipal facilities and their bondholders.

In 1994, the U.S. Supreme Court also ruled that an environmental requirement that a landowner dedicate to the public a bicycle path as a condition for development of property constituted a "taking" which constitutionally entitled the landowner to fair compensation. *Dolan v. City of Tigard*, 114 S. Ct. 2309 (1994). In 1994, the federal government was also ordered by the U.S. Court of Claims to pay a property owner for loss of value after the U.S. Army Corps of Engineers denied a fill permit for installation of a septic system at a residential lot, thus destroying the only economically viable use of the property. *Bowles v. United States*, 31 Fed. Ct. 37 (1994). See also *Creppel v. U.S.*, 41 F.2d 627 (Fed. Civ. 1994).

XXIII. STATE LAWS

A.   State General Environmental Laws

As explained earlier, with a few exceptions, the states have adopted laws implementing the major federal environmental laws and have appointed agencies to administer and enforce them. The agencies have adopted regulations implementing the state laws and have generally been successful in obtaining approval from the USEPA for their programs. Thus, in most states, regulation of the programs established by the CAA, CWA, SDWA, RCRA and other laws is administered by the state agencies.

While the state programs generally follow the federal patterns, there are numerous differences which reflect historical developments and adaptations to local conditions. Thus, it is beyond the scope of this book to attempt to cover the multitude of state laws and regulations.

However, the reader should be aware that most state environmental agencies are major, fully staffed organizations with considerable expertise and experience. They typically have headquarters in the state capitol where senior administration, and perhaps also central engineering and laboratory facilities, are located. They also have regional, district and/or local offices which perform inspection, enforcement and other functions.

XXIII. STATE LAWS

The state environmental agencies often assume a leadership role in regional, state or local matters where their "hands on" experience may provide more insight than is available to the USEPA. For example, the Pennsylvania Department of Environmental Resources has developed streamlined permitting methods applicable to companies which produce a wide and changing variety of chemical products. The Illinois Pollution Control Board has established regulation, for categories of special wastes which require more management than ordinary solid wastes, but less management than hazardous wastes, thus providing an economical waste disposal alternative. The Minnesota Department of Natural Resources sponsored special disposal methods for wastes resulting from abatement of lead-based paint.

The New Jersey Department of Environmental Protection, once known primarily for its strict enforcement policies, has in recent years developed a number of leading programs designed to facilitate compliance. For example, it has adopted and published technical criteria for site investigation and remediation. It has also published residential and nonresidential soil and groundwater cleanup criteria. Under memoranda of understanding which require cost reimbursement at reasonable rates, the Department provides review of compliance work including site investigation and remediation plans. These reviews often benefit from the considerable expertise of its laboratory and quality control personnel who maintain contact with the advanced environmental programs of the USEPA at Research Triangle Park, North Carolina and elsewhere.

A number of states have established statutory programs to provide funding for cleanup of leaks from underground storage tanks. However, these programs have been only partially successful because applications for funds have exceeded the needs anticipated when the programs were established. Thus, the state environmental agencies administering these programs have found it necessary to apply the limited available resources to situations having relatively high priority.

B. Real Estate Transfer Laws

A few states have adopted laws which require that industrial and commercial real property must be inspected for contamination with hazardous substances at the time of a sale and certain other transfers. Transfers which may create a cleanup obligation include a change in ownership of a corporation or other entity which owns or operates the property, a lease expiration, a bankruptcy, or a shutdown or curtailment of operations.

For example, even a sale of corporate ownership by out-of-state shareholders or a merger may require compliance with a law such as the New Jersey Industrial Site Recovery Act (ISRA). In New Jersey, ISRA provides that an owner or operator planning to close operations or to sell or transfer ownership or operations of an industrial establishment classified under certain standard industrial codes (if minimal hazardous substance activities have taken place) must file a notice and a negative declaration with the Department of Environmental Protection (DEP). If the property is not contaminated, the owner or operator can submit appropriate information and request approval of the negative declaration by the DEP. If the property is contaminated, an investigation must be conducted and a cleanup plan must be prepared in accordance with the DEP's technical requirements for site remediation and approved by the DEP. The owner or operator must agree to reimburse the DEP's surveillance costs. A letter of credit, bond, trust fund or other evidence of financial responsibility must be provided to assure performance of the cleanup. The DEP will allow a transfer of the property once it has satisfactory assurances for the cleanup. When the cleanup is performed in compliance with the technical requirements, the DEP will approve a negative declaration. ISRA contains several exemptions under which the cleanup obligation may be excused, deferred or limited, but almost all of them require DEPE approval which is difficult to obtain. An attempt to close operations, sell or transfer without compliance is voidable by the buyer or the DEP and punishable by fines. 13 NJSA § 13:1K-6 *et seq.*

In Connecticut, the Transfer Act does not void a sale, but requires the seller of an establishment where hazardous substances have been used to provide to the buyer prior to the sale a negative declaration concerning hazardous wastes at the property. A copy must be filed with the Department of Environmental Protection within 15 days after the sale. If the property is contaminated, the buyer (or another responsible person such as the seller) must certify to the Department of Environmental Protection that it will take cleanup action as required by the Department. Noncompliance renders the seller liable to the buyer and to fines. 22a Conn. Gen. Stat. Annot., § 22a - 134 *et seq.*

The State of Indiana has an Environmental Hazardous Disclosure and Responsible Party Transfer Law which requires disclosure of environmental defects to buyers. 13 Indiana Code § 13-7-22.5-1 *et seq.* The State of Illinois has a Responsible Property Transfer Act that requires delivery of a document disclosing environmental information to buyers and a copy is filed with the Illinois Environmental Protection Agency. 765 ILCS, § 90/1 *et seq.* See also California Health and Safety Code, § 25359.7 and Michigan Compiled Laws Annot., § 699.610c.

Some state laws grant to the state environmental agency a lien or a "superlien" securing cleanup costs expended by the agency for abandoned or other hazardous waste sites. The lien or superlien may apply to the property where the costs were incurred and perhaps also to other properties of the owner or operator. The superlien law should be reviewed to determine the extent to which it may have priority over mortgages and security interests held by banks and other lenders including those recorded before the inception of the superlien. For example, see Maine Rev. Stat. Annot., Title 38, § 1371 and Mass. Gen. Laws Annot., Vol. 2B, Chap. 21E, § 13, (1993 Supp. Pamphlet).

XXIV. FUTURE TRENDS

In addition to their specific objectives, the environmental laws and regulations are part of the political, social and economic history and future of the U.S. Like other nations, the U.S. has benefitted greatly from industrial and scientific development. However, while solving the problems of its own and prior generations, each generation fails to foresee some needs of future generations.

The most important result of the environmental laws may be the requirement that foresight be applied to the environment.

Past generations did not wholly ignore the environment as environmentalists tend to believe. They saw its imminent and chronic hazards in their daily lives. The author recommends that readers interested in earlier perceptions of the environment read "On the Banks of Plum Creek," Laura Ingalls Wilder, Harper & Row and particularly Chapter 25, "The Glittering Cloud" and the following Chapters. These Chapters show the harsh impacts of the natural environment which made people welcome pesticides, fertilizers and other developments which sheltered them from the environment.

After the great depression and "dust storms" of the 1930's followed by World War II, the people of the U.S. were glad to turn their efforts to industry and science. They achieved an abundance of food, effective medicines, affordable clothing and housing, education, high speed travel and communication, and many other improvements of living conditions previously unknown in the U.S. and other nations except to wealthy people. However, development came so fast that few saw its environmental side effects which harmed human health and the environment. Thus, the environmental laws and regulations were needed.

During the first 25 years, the environmental laws were applied primarily to private industry. However, as environmental government agencies have sought to require compliance by federal, state and municipal governments and by the general public, they have encountered criticism and demands which private industry could not effectively make. Three demands have gained the greatest priority. The first is to establish realistic risk assessment methods. The second is to match regulatory mandates with funding to pay for compliance. The third is to provide fair compensation to persons whose property is taken in order to achieve environmental objectives.

The USEPA assesses risk by very conservative methods. For example, the USEPA sometimes applies repeated significant uncertainty factor adjustments when calculating a reference dose from no observed and lowest observed adverse effect level data derived from laboratory small animal tests. Further, the USEPA determines cancer risk by linear extrapolation from exposure dose to carcinogenic response, however small the dose, while deriving data from tests in which laboratory animals are force fed chemicals for their lifetimes at levels higher than humans could tolerate even briefly. In addition, the EPA uses upper bound interpretation of sampling data and may assume up to 70 years of exposure to hazards without evidence that anyone would actually be exposed for even a fraction of the period selected. When using "worst case" analysis, the USEPA assumes cases which go beyond the worst real events to theoretical events.

The public understands that government agencies should include a reasonable margin for error in their standards. However, there is growing objection to overstatement of risk by many orders of magnitude. There is also a growing public belief that environmental laws and regulations should be subject to reasonable cost/benefit analysis and that regulatory programs found beneficial to the public should be funded when adopted.

With bipartisan support, Congress is considering several bills to require the USEPA to evaluate risk by sounder scientific methods, require cost/benefit analysis, require funding for requirements imposed on state and municipal governments and compensate property owners for loss of value created by the environmental laws. If adopted, these legislative reforms should strengthen the environmental laws by enhancing public confidence and allocating resources more realistically to protect human health and the environment.

In addition, a wide range of other legislative, regulatory and court actions are in progress. Among the most important legislative efforts in 1995 will be reauthorization of the SWDA and CERCLA, both of which were nearly enacted in 1994. The tax which funds the "Superfund" under CERCLA is scheduled to expire on December 31, 1995, a factor which should provide impetus to reach the compromises necessary to amend CERCLA. Legislation to amend the CWA has also been introduced.

Other programs of public interest include the USEPA's plans to revise its stormwater and storage tank programs to make them operate more effectively.

XXV. CONCLUSION

In conclusion, the author hopes that this book will provide to its readers a convenient tool to become acquainted with the U.S. environmental laws and reference sources where further information can be found. More than most other nations, the U.S. prefers to be governed by laws (and regulations) rather than the judgmental decisions of persons holding government responsibilities. Thus, effort devoted to understanding the laws and regulations is worthwhile because, once adopted, they are widely followed by those who regulate and those who are regulated, regardless of their personal beliefs. The author also hopes that the book well illustrates the process of change that is characteristic of U.S. laws and regulations because the general attitude of compliance depends significantly on freedom to seek change through legislative, regulatory and judicial processes.

Edward E. Shea, Esq.

June 1995